# ClearRevise®

## Edexcel GCSE
## History 1HI0

Illustrated revision and practice

Option P4:
Superpower relations and the Cold War, 1941–91

**Published by**
PG Online Limited
The Old Coach House
35 Main Road
Tolpuddle
Dorset
DT2 7EW
United Kingdom

sales@pgonline.co.uk
www.clearrevise.com
www.pgonline.co.uk
**2022**

**PG** ONLINE

# PREFACE

Absolute clarity! That's the aim.

This is everything you need to ace the Period Study component of Paper 2 and beam with pride. Each topic is laid out in a beautifully illustrated format that is clear, approachable and as concise and simple as possible.

Each section of the specification is clearly indicated to help you cross-reference your revision. The checklist on the contents pages will help you keep track of what you have already worked through and what's left before the big day.

We have included worked exam-style questions with answers. There is also a set of exam-style questions at the end of each section for you to practise writing answers. You can check your answers against those given at the end of the book.

# LEVELS OF LEARNING

Based on the degree to which you are able to truly understand a new topic, we recommend that you work in stages. Start by reading a short explanation of something, then try and recall what you've just read. This will have limited effect if you stop there but it aids the next stage. Question everything. Write down your own summary and then complete and mark a related exam-style question. Cover up the answers if necessary but learn from them once you've seen them. Lastly, teach someone else. Explain the topic in a way that they can understand. Have a go at the different practice questions – they offer an insight into how and where marks are awarded.

Design and artwork: Jessica Webb / PG Online Ltd

First edition 2022   10 9 8 7 6 5 4 3 2 1
A catalogue entry for this book is available from the British Library
ISBN: 978-1-910523-45-2
Copyright © PG Online 2022

Printed on FSC certified paper by Bell and Bain Ltd, Glasgow, UK.

# THE SCIENCE OF REVISION

## Illustrations and words

Research has shown that revising with words and pictures doubles the quality of responses by students.[1] This is known as 'dual-coding' because it provides two ways of fetching the information from our brain. The improvement in responses is particularly apparent in students when they are asked to apply their knowledge to different problems. Recall, application and judgement are all specifically and carefully assessed in public examination questions.

## Retrieval of information

Retrieval practice encourages students to come up with answers to questions.[2] The closer the question is to one you might see in a real examination, the better. Also, the closer the environment in which a student revises is to the 'examination environment', the better. Students who had a test 2–7 days away did 30% better using retrieval practice than students who simply read, or repeatedly reread material. Students who were expected to teach the content to someone else after their revision period did better still.[3] What was found to be most interesting in other studies is that students using retrieval methods and testing for revision were also more resilient to the introduction of stress.[4]

## Ebbinghaus' forgetting curve and spaced learning

Ebbinghaus' 140-year-old study examined the rate at which we forget things over time. The findings still hold true. However, the act of forgetting facts and techniques and relearning them is what cements them into the brain.[5] Spacing out revision is more effective than cramming – we know that, but students should also know that the space between revisiting material should vary depending on how far away the examination is. A cyclical approach is required. An examination 12 months away necessitates revisiting covered material about once a month. A test in 30 days should have topics revisited every 3 days – intervals of roughly a tenth of the time available.[6]

## Summary

Students: the more tests and past questions you do, in an environment as close to examination conditions as possible, the better you are likely to perform on the day. If you prefer to listen to music while you revise, tunes without lyrics will be far less detrimental to your memory and retention. Silence is most effective.[5] If you choose to study with friends, choose carefully – effort is contagious.[7]

1.      Mayer, R. E., & Anderson, R. B. (1991). Animations need narrations: An experimental test of dual-coding hypothesis. *Journal of Education Psychology*, (83)4, 484–490.

2.      Roediger III, H. L., & Karpicke, J.D. (2006). Test-enhanced learning: Taking memory tests improves long-term retention. *Psychological Science*, 17(3), 249–255.

3.      Nestojko, J., Bui, D., Kornell, N. & Bjork, E. (2014). Expecting to teach enhances learning and organisation of knowledge in free recall of text passages. *Memory and Cognition*, 42(7), 1038–1048.

4.      Smith, A. M., Floerke, V. A., & Thomas, A. K. (2016) Retrieval practice protects memory against acute stress. *Science*, 354(6315), 1046–1048.

5.      Perham, N., & Currie, H. (2014). Does listening to preferred music improve comprehension performance? *Applied Cognitive Psychology*, 28(2), 279–284.

6.      Cepeda, N. J., Vul, E., Rohrer, D., Wixted, J. T. & Pashler, H. (2008). Spacing effects in learning a temporal ridgeline of optimal retention. *Psychological Science*, 19(11), 1095–1102.

7.      Busch, B. & Watson, E. (2019), *The Science of Learning*, 1st ed. Routledge.

# CONTENTS

## Option P4 Superpower relations and the Cold War, 1941–91

## Key topic 1 The origins of the Cold War, 1941–58

## Key topic 2 Cold War crises, 1958–70

**Specification point** ☑

# MARK ALLOCATIONS

All the questions in this book require extended responses. These answers should be marked in accordance with the levels-based mark schemes on pages 52 and 53. The answers provided are examples only. There are many more points to make than there are marks available, so the answers are not exhaustive.

## Understanding the specification reference tabs

This number refers to the key topic. In this example, *Cold War crises, 1958–70.*

This number refers to the bullet point. In this example, *The refugee problem in Berlin.*

**2.1.1**

This number refers to the subtopic. In this example, *Increased tension between East and West.*

# THE EXAM

Paper 2 is split across two booklets. Booklet P is the Period Study and Booklet B is the British Depth Study. This revision guide covers Booklet P4. The questions follow the same format every year, so make sure you're familiar with them before the big day.

### Q1  'Explain two consequences of...'

This question tests your understanding of **consequence** (the result of something). This question is worth 8 marks. You need to suggest two consequences and support each of them with specific information and evidence to get full marks.

### Q2  'Write a narrative account analysing the key events of...'

To do well in this question you've got to do more than just reel off a list of events. You also need to demonstrate understanding of **causation**, **consequence** and **change** and the events need to be organised into a clear sequence which reach an outcome. You'll be provided with two stimulus points in the question, but to get top marks you also need to include information that goes beyond the stimulus points. This question is worth 8 marks.

### Q3  'Explain two of the following. The importance of... for...'

This question will give you the option of three events or policies. You only need to write about two, and each option is worth 8 marks. This question tests your understanding of **consequence** and **significance** (why something happened and why it was important). You need to structure your answer to show clear reasoning, and use supporting evidence to justify your answer.

# TOPICS FOR PAPER 2
## PERIOD STUDY

Option P4:
Superpower relations
and the Cold War, 1941–91

## Information about Paper 2

**Written exam: 1 hour 45 minutes (This includes the British depth study)**
**64 marks (32 marks for each of the British depth study and the period study)**
**40% of the qualification grade (20% for each of the British depth study and the period study)**

**Specification coverage**

Key topic 1: The origins of the Cold War, 1941–58

Key topic 2: Cold War crises, 1958–70

Key topic 3: The end of the Cold War, 1970–91

**Questions**

Answer question 1 and 2, as well as two options from question 3.

# THE GRAND ALLIANCE AND CONFERENCES

During World War II, the USA, Soviet Union and Britain fought together against Nazi Germany. Even before the war ended, it was clear that relations between the Western powers and the Soviet Union would not stay friendly.

## The Grand Alliance

In 1941, the USA, Soviet Union and Britain formed the **Grand Alliance** to defeat Germany and Japan during World War II. They agreed to work together but their relationship was uneasy:

- The only thing the countries had in common was their desire to win the war.
- The Western Powers and the Soviet Union (also known as the **USSR**) had ideological differences. The West was **capitalist**, and the Soviet Union was **communist** (see **page 4**). Their differences made them suspicious of each other.

In 1941, the USSR was made up of modern-day Russia along with 14 other Soviet Republics, such as modern-day Estonia, Latvia, Belarus and Ukraine.

## The Yalta Conference, Feb 1945

By 1945, it looked likely the **Allies** (Britain, the USSR and the USA) would win the war. At the Yalta Conference, the Grand Alliance discussed what should happen after the war ended.

### Agreement

- To split Germany into four zones. France, Britain, the USA and the USSR would each control a zone.
- To force Germany to pay **reparations** (repayments to other countries for the cost of the war).
- To set up the **United Nations** (a peace-keeping organisation).
- To have free elections in the countries of Eastern Europe that had been liberated from Nazi control.

## The Tehran Conference, 1943

The Grand Alliance met in Tehran, 1943. They discussed an invasion of Nazi-occupied France. Stalin, the leader of the USSR, wanted British and American troops to fight the Nazis on a second front in Europe, to ease the pressure on his **Red Army** fighting the Nazis on the eastern front.

### Agreement

The USA and Britain would invade France in 1944, and the USSR would join the war against Japan after the Nazis were defeated.

### Concerns

It was not agreed what should happen to Germany after the war.

### Concerns

There were disagreements over how Poland should be run after the war (Poland had been occupied by Nazi Germany). These disagreements made it clear that it would be difficult for the West and the USSR to agree how Eastern Europe should be governed.

# The Potsdam Conference, July 1945

The Potsdam Conference happened after Germany surrendered. As the leaders discussed the post-war situation, it became clear that relations between the USSR and the West were strained. Truman replaced Roosevelt as the US President and he had a much more hard-line approach to the USSR.

## Agreement

- To divide Germany into four zones. Berlin, Germany's capital, was in the USSR's zone, but it was also split into four zones and shared between France, Britain, the USA and the USSR.
- To let the controlling power in each zone take reparations in kind from its zone.

## Concerns

- Stalin had made sure Poland's government was pro-communist. The USA and Britain were concerned that Stalin did not intend to allow the free elections in Eastern Europe that had been agreed at Yalta.
- Stalin insisted that Germany pay the Soviet Union higher amounts of reparations to compensate for Soviet losses during the war, but the other members of the Grand Alliance refused.

Great Britain

USSR

USA

France

**Division of Germany**

Truman told Stalin about the USA's atomic bomb at Potsdam (page 7). This made Stalin feel threatened and tensions worsened.

Explain **two** consequences of the Potsdam Conference. [8]

> One consequence was that it was finally decided what should happen to Germany after the war. It was to be divided into four zones, one administered by the USSR, one by the USA, one by France and one by Britain. Berlin was divided in a similar way, even though it was in the Soviet-controlled zone. The division of Germany and Berlin between the West and the USSR would create tensions throughout the Cold War.
>
> A second consequence was that the mistrust and suspicion that existed between the USA and Stalin increased. Stalin had promised free elections in Poland during the Yalta conference, but the Western allies left the Potsdam Conference doubting that he would really allow this because Stalin had installed a pro-communist government in Poland.

*This question should be marked in accordance with the levels-based mark scheme on page 52.*

**Division of Berlin**

The USSR was determined to create an area of countries which were friendly to the USSR on Germany's border, such as Poland. This is sometimes called the **buffer zone** (page 8) because these countries acted as a buffer between the USSR and the West.

# IDEOLOGICAL DIFFERENCES

The USA was a capitalist country, whereas the Soviet Union was communist.

## Ideological differences between the superpowers

### Capitalism

- Everyone in society should be free to invest their money and to own land, businesses and property. They should be able to keep any profits they make.
- There should be **democracy**. Free elections with a choice of political parties.
- Some people would become more important than others because of their family background or wealth and achievements.

### Communism

- All land and businesses should be owned by the state and any profits made should be used for the good of all. There should be no individual profit making.
- There should be elections, but candidates should all be from the same party.
- All citizens should be equal.

The USA and the USSR didn't just have different beliefs, they bitterly opposed each other's beliefs. The USSR believed the USA wanted to wipe out communism, and the USA thought that the USSR wanted to spread communism to all countries and destroy their democratic, capitalist system.

American propaganda showing the threat of communism (left), and Russian propaganda showing the greed of capitalism (right).

## Attitudes of Stalin, Truman and Churchill

**Joseph Stalin**

Stalin wanted to take any steps necessary to make the USSR strong enough to defend itself from the USA and Britain. He was deeply suspicious of the West.

**Harry S. Truman**

Truman became US President in April 1945. He was much less trusting of the USSR than Roosevelt had been and was determined to adopt a hard-line approach towards the USSR in negotiations.

**Winston Churchill**

Churchill was deeply suspicious of Stalin and was the first to talk of an **Iron Curtain** (see page 8). Churchill lost his position as British Prime Minister in 1945.

Britain was in decline at this time, so it was the USA and the USSR who dominated world affairs from 1945. They became known as **superpowers**.

## The Cold War

The Grand Alliance dissolved after World War II. The distrust between the superpowers and their fear of each other led to the **Cold War**. This wasn't a war that used soldiers and weapons, instead, the two superpowers were bitter rivals who tried to extend their influence and win diplomatic victories over each other by:

| building up their militaries | using propaganda | controlling other countries | helping other countries with aid | spying on each other |
|---|---|---|---|---|
|  |  |  |  |  |

Neither the USSR nor the USA wanted outright war. Both sides had just emerged from World War II and did not want to start another conflict against each other.

Write a narrative account analysing the Grand Alliance in the years c1943–1945.

You **may** use the following in your answer:

- the Tehran Conference, 1943
- the Yalta Conference, 1945

You **must** also use your own knowledge. [8]

*The Grand Alliance was formed between the USA, Britain and the USSR to try to defeat Nazi Germany in World War II. The Grand Alliance met at the Tehran Conference (1943) and agreed that Britain and the USA would ease pressure on USSR's Red Army fighting Germany on the eastern front by creating a second front in the west. Stalin also agreed to join the fight against Japan. This suggested the countries of the Grand Alliance were prepared to work together to defeat Germany.*

*The Grand Alliance had been successful in working together to defeat Nazi Germany, and they met again at the Yalta Conference (1945) to discuss what might happen after the war. They agreed that Germany should be split into four zones, and a zone would be controlled by the USSR, the USA, Britain and France. It was also agreed that the countries of Eastern Europe which had been liberated from Nazi control should have free elections to allow the people to decide how their countries should be run. However, there were disagreements about how Poland should be governed after the war, which made it clear that there would be tensions between the USSR and the West with regards to how Eastern Europe should be governed.*

*The Grand Alliance met again at the Potsdam Conference (1945) after Germany surrendered, to discuss the post-war situation. It was clear at this conference that relations between the USSR and the West were strained. The Grand Alliance agreed to split Berlin into four zones, each to be controlled by France, the USSR, the USA and Britain. Each controlling nation could also take reparations from its zone, but Stalin wanted higher reparations to account for Soviet losses in the war. However, the other nations disagreed. This demonstrated that tensions were beginning to worsen between East and West. Furthermore, the Western Allies were concerned that Stalin did not intend to allow free elections in Poland, as he had established a pro-communist government. This went against what had been agreed at Yalta, and increased tension and suspicion between the West and the USSR. The Grand Alliance was dissolved following the end of the Second World War which suggested that the countries weren't prepared to co-operate once Germany had been defeated.*

*This question should be marked in accordance with the levels-based mark scheme on page 52.*

To get top marks, you need to include information other than the bullet points in the question.

# THE ATOMIC BOMB AND THE LONG AND NOVIKOV TELEGRAMS

Following the end of the war, tensions between the USSR and the USA continued to mount.

## The development of the atomic bomb

Even after Germany surrendered in May 1945, Japan continued to fight. In August 1945, the USA dropped atomic bombs on the Japanese cities of Hiroshima and Nagasaki. The bombs brought an end to the war, but they also meant that the USA didn't need Soviet help to defeat Japan.

In August 1945, the USSR did not have an atomic bomb, so when Truman met Stalin at Potsdam, he felt the USA had an advantage over the USSR. However, this advantage did not last long.

- Stalin knew (through spies) the USA had an atomic bomb and Soviet scientists were developing their own. This was ready in August 1949, triggering an **arms race** (page 15) where each country tried to develop more powerful weapons than the other.

- The threat of nuclear weapons made Stalin even more determined to build a pro-Soviet buffer zone between Germany and the Soviet Union (**page 8**).

The ruins of Nagasaki after the atomic bomb.

## The Long and Novikov telegrams

In 1946, both the USA and the USSR asked for reports on their rivals.

### The Long Telegram

George Keenan, the US ambassador in Moscow, sent President Truman a telegram saying the Soviet Union was heavily armed and wanted to destroy capitalism to protect its communist system. The telegram confirmed that the USSR was a threat to world peace, and only strong action by the USA would stop the USSR.

### The Novikov telegram

Nikolai Novikov, a Soviet diplomat in Washington, reported to his government that the USA wanted to take over the world. If that meant going to war with the USSR to destroy communism, then that would happen. The USSR needed to find ways to stop this.

The telegrams confirmed each country's worst-case scenario and contributed to mounting tensions.

# THE CREATION OF SOVIET SATELLITE STATES IN EASTERN EUROPE

Even before the Grand Alliance ended, Stalin had been establishing 'satellite' states on his western border to protect the USSR from attack.

## Soviet satellite states

During the Second World War, Soviet troops had advanced through Eastern Europe to reach Germany. Stalin decided to keep some of the territory his troops had captured and made sure he had governments which supported him in Poland, Hungary, Romania, Czechoslovakia and Bulgaria. By 1948, he had set up his buffer zone in Eastern Europe using these **satellite states** (countries that were technically independent but were heavily influenced by the USSR) which is also known as Stalin's **sphere of influence**. Many people in these countries were unhappy with Soviet control but faced oppression if they objected (see **page 16** and **page 32**).

A Polish anti-Soviet poster showing Stalin as a spider.

This group of countries is also known as the **Eastern Bloc**.

## The Iron Curtain

During the Cold War, it was common for people in Western Europe to talk about countries being 'behind the Iron Curtain'. This phrase came from a speech made by Winston Churchill in March 1946. The Iron Curtain was the border between pro-capitalist European countries in the west, and pro-communist countries in the east.

The Yugoslavian leader, Tito, refused to follow instructions from Stalin, but his government was communist and so not a threat to the USSR.

A map showing the Eastern Bloc countries (which formed the USSR's buffer zone). The imaginary political boundary of the Iron Curtain lies along the border of the Eastern Bloc.

# THE TRUMAN DOCTRINE AND THE MARSHALL PLAN

Many European countries were weak after World War II. The USA was concerned they would turn to communism to solve their economic problems.

## The Truman Doctrine, 1947

Worried by the potential spread of communism, President Truman promised aid to any country which was threatened by communism. This aid could be diplomatic, financial or military.

The Communist Party was gaining support in Turkey and Greece, so the USA sent millions of dollars to combat the spread of communism.

Previously, the USA had followed a policy of **isolationism** so they avoided getting involved with international affairs. However, this couldn't continue if the USA wanted to control communism abroad. Instead, the USA adopted a policy of **containment** which meant they would get involved in world affairs to stop communism from spreading.

## The Marshall Plan, 1947

An American General, George Marshall, was sent to Europe to suggest ways to stop communism from spreading. He advised Truman to spend $12 billion to help the European economy recover after the war. This **Marshall Aid** was effectively a form of propaganda to show Europe that they didn't need communism and that capitalism would help them rebuild following the war.

## Impact of the Marshall Plan

Sixteen countries received Marshall Aid, with Britain, France and Western-controlled Germany receiving the most. Turkey also received aid and allowed the USA to build missile bases on its land which would be significant for the **Cuban Missile Crisis** (page 26).

The Soviet Union refused to accept any money from the Marshall Plan, and blocked its satellite states, such as Poland and Romania, from receiving aid. The USSR worried that accepting American money would make communist countries reliant on the West, as well as weakening communism in the Eastern Bloc.

By the early 1950s, most western European economies had begun to recover. In France and Italy, this led to a drop in support of communism as living standards improved. The Marshall Plan was successful in preventing the spread of communism and created allies in Europe for the USA.

MARSHALL·PLAN

A propaganda poster showing support for the Marshall Plan in Europe. ERP stands for European Recovery Programme.

# COMINFORM AND COMECON

Stalin was angered by the Truman Doctrine and the Marshall Plan and thought the USA was trying to buy influence in Europe. The USSR responded with Cominform and Comecon.

## Cominform, 1947

**Cominform** (the Communist Information Bureau) was a direct response to the Truman Doctrine. It aimed to strengthen communism by placing all the European communist parties under the control of the USSR. It attempted to create a trade network between communist countries (to prevent them trading with capitalist countries in the West) and published a newspaper to spread communist ideas.

## Comecon, 1949

**Comecon** (the Council for Mutual Economic Assistance) aimed to **centralise** the planning of industry and agriculture in the Eastern Bloc (bring Eastern Bloc industry and agriculture under the control of the Soviet Union). It also promised financial aid to keep the Eastern Bloc countries loyal to communism. This was called the **Molotov Plan** and was a direct response to the Marshall Plan.

An American cartoon from 1951 showing Stalin on top of the world with communist countries on his cape.

The West formed a military alliance in 1949 called **NATO** (page 14).

## The impact of Cominform and Comecon

Cominform and Comecon strengthened the USSR's ties with countries in its sphere of influence. The introduction of the Molotov Plan satisfied those countries who had been prohibited from accepting aid from the Marshall Plan.

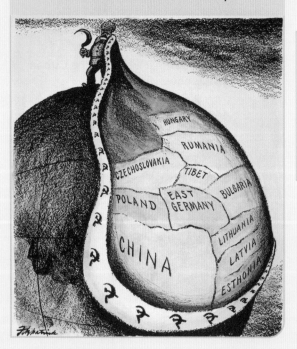

1. Explain **two** consequences of the Marshall Plan. [8]
2. Explain the importance of the Truman Doctrine for tensions between the USA and the USSR. [8]

1. *One consequence of the Marshall Plan was that sixteen European countries received financial aid from America. This money helped to boost European industries which had suffered during World War II. This had the effect of preventing communism from spreading in Europe, as living standards improved and countries who received the aid saw the benefits of a capitalist system. These Marshall Aid countries also became allied to the USA.*

   *A second consequence of the Marshall Plan was that the USSR created their own version, called the Molotov Plan which was devised by Comecon. The USSR wanted to create a rival programme to the Marshall Plan to keep up with the USA and show the strength of communism. This was especially important since Stalin had forbidden Eastern Bloc countries from accepting Marshall Aid, and he needed to offer an equivalent system to keep those countries loyal.*

2. *President Truman was worried by the potential spread of communism in Europe, especially following World War II when many European countries had suffered economically. He was concerned that communism's policies of equality and shared wealth would seem attractive to those people who had been devastated by the war. Truman introduced the Truman Doctrine to try to address this, which promised aid to any country that was threatened by communism. This aid could be financial, military or diplomatic. Truman gave Greece and Turkey a substantial amount of money as part of the Truman Doctrine to prevent communism from spreading there, which was especially important as these countries were very close to the Eastern Bloc.*

   *The introduction of the Truman Doctrine angered the USSR. Stalin felt that the USA was trying to buy influence in Europe as well as demonstrating the power of capitalism, which made the USSR feel threatened. In response, the USSR introduced Cominform, which aimed to put all the European communist parties under the control of the USSR. It aimed to strengthen relationships between communist countries by developing a trade network and published a newspaper to spread communist ideas. This behaviour of the USSR introducing rival policies in response to Western policies was central to the continuation of the Cold War, as neither country wanted to be dominated by the other.*

*These questions should be marked in accordance with the levels-based mark scheme on pages 52-53.*

# THE BERLIN CRISIS, 1948–49

Germany had been split into 4 zones. The USA, France, the USSR and Britain each controlled a zone. Berlin, Germany's capital, was in the middle of the USSR's zone.

## Berlin's zones

Even though Berlin was in the USSR's zone, it too was split into four zones, with the USSR, the USA, France and Britain each controlling part of it. For the USA, France and Britain to get to their zones, they needed to travel through USSR-controlled territory. They could access Berlin via road, rail, canal and air corridors (restricted airspace for planes).

## The Berlin Blockade

Stalin wanted Germany to remain weak, so it could act as another 'buffer' country between the USSR and the West, but the West were helping their German zones to rebuild:

- The USA had given Germany money as part of the Marshall Plan.
- The USA provided German shopkeepers with goods to stimulate their economy.
- The West had stabilised the currency in the zones they controlled.
- In 1948 the British, American and French zones joined together and were called 'Trizonia'. The unified zones became known as **West Germany** in May 1949.

Stalin felt threatened by the actions of the West, and worried that they would try to invade the USSR-controlled part of Berlin. On 24th June 1948, Stalin decided to assert his authority over Soviet-controlled Germany by denying the USA, Britain and France land access to their zones in Berlin. Stalin hoped that this would lead the Western powers to withdraw from West Berlin. This became known as the **Berlin Blockade**.

Map showing air access to Berlin.

## Impact of the Blockade on West Berlin

The Western-controlled part of Berlin, known as **West Berlin**, could now only be reached by air. Supplies that had previously arrived by land dried up, and West Berlin faced a shortage of food, fuel and medicine.

The West refused to withdraw from Berlin, and instead flew supplies into West Berlin, which became known as the **Berlin Airlift**. The airlift lasted for 11 months, at a cost of approximately $224 million to the West. On 12th May 1949, the land blockade was lifted by the USSR.

Berliners watching supplies land at Tempelhof Airport, 1948.

## Consequences of the Berlin Blockade

### Worsening relations

The Berlin Blockade was the first outright show of hostilities between the superpowers, and highlighted Germany and Berlin as a point of tension. Lifting the blockade was a source of humiliation for Stalin, and a victory for the West.

### The Federal Republic of Germany and German Democratic Republic

Even after the Berlin Blockade, Berlin remained divided. In 1949, the West announced the formation of the **Federal Republic of Germany** (West Germany), and democratic elections were held in August. The elections were won by an anti-communist candidate. East Germany became known as the **German Democratic Republic**.

### Migration

After the Berlin Blockade, more Germans living in East Berlin and East Germany migrated into Western-controlled areas (see **page 19**).

Hostilities over Berlin and an increase in migration eventually led to the **Berlin Wall** (see page 22).

### Promoting capitalism

The West used the high numbers of refugees leaving East Germany in their propaganda. They claimed the migration was due to a lack of human rights in Soviet-controlled East Germany.

---

Explain **two** consequences of the Berlin Blockade. [8]

*One consequence of the Berlin Blockade was worsening relations between the superpowers. The Berlin Blockade attempted to cut off West Berlin from the Western Allies by denying them access through Soviet-controlled East Germany. This was the first open show of hostilities between the USA and the USSR. The blockade was lifted by the USSR after 11 months, which humiliated the Soviet Union and led to further tension.*

*Another consequence was that Germans living in East Berlin realised that the USSR was willing to take extreme measures to control the people living in its zone. As a result, many people decided to escape the East and migrate into West-controlled areas of Germany. The West were very willing to allow this, as it demonstrated that Germans preferred capitalism over communism and the West used this migration in their propaganda as an example of capitalism being superior to communism.*

*This question should be marked in accordance with the levels-based mark scheme on page 52.*

# NATO AND THE WARSAW PACT

The Berlin Crisis had proven that the USSR was prepared to be openly hostile towards the West. As a result, the West created NATO and the USSR retaliated by creating the Warsaw Pact.

### The formation of NATO

In April 1949, **NATO** (North Atlantic Treaty Organisation) was created by the Western powers, including Britain, the USA, France, Italy, Greece, Turkey, Norway and Canada. It was a military alliance which agreed if one member of the organisation came under attack, the other member states would help protect it.

An American cartoon from 1949 showing a Soviet soldier. A caption beneath the original cartoon reads "Banner of the Non-Soviet Union".

### The Warsaw Pact

The USSR felt threatened by the formation of NATO and decided to create their own version in 1955. The **Warsaw Pact** brought together the USSR and the Eastern Bloc countries to form their own military alliance.

### The impact of NATO and the Warsaw Pact

NATO and the Warsaw Pact created two opposing military alliances and forced other countries to pick a side. This increased Cold War tensions as there were now two power blocs.

NATO and the Warsaw Pact also contributed to the arms race (**page 15**). Both military alliances needed more powerful weaponry to protect their members in case of outright war.

The Warsaw Pact became a flashpoint for the Hungarian Uprising in 1956 (**page 16**) and it became clear that Eastern Bloc countries would be punished for attempting to leave the Pact.

# THE ARMS RACE

Throughout the 1940s–60s, the USSR and USA tried to out-do each other with weapons. This is known as the **arms race**.

**1945** – the USA drops atomic bombs on Hiroshima and Nagasaki.

**1949** – the USSR creates its own atomic bomb. The USA is no longer the only country with nuclear weapons.

**1952** – the USA tests the first **Hydrogen bomb**, which was up to 1,000 times more powerful than the atomic bomb.

**1953** – the USSR tests its own Hydrogen bomb.

**1954** – the USA announces a **Doctrine of Massive Retaliation**. This states that any attack on the USA or its allies would result in retaliation much more severe than the initial attack.

**1957** – the USSR creates the first **ICBM** (Intercontinental Ballistic Missile), a rocket able to carry a nuclear warhead thousands of miles.

**1961** – the USSR tests the Tsar Bomba, the most powerful hydrogen bomb ever created.

**1959** – the USA develops an ICBM.

**1959** – the USA sends submarines capable of launching nuclear weapons to the coast of the USSR.

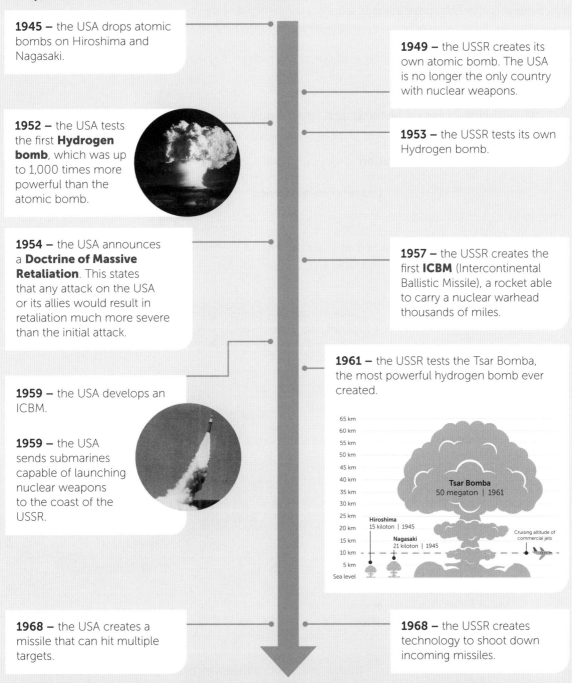

65 km
60 km
55 km
50 km
45 km
40 km
35 km
30 km
25 km
20 km
15 km
10 km
5 km
Sea level

**Tsar Bomba**
50 megaton | 1961

Hiroshima
15 kiloton | 1945

Nagasaki
21 kiloton | 1945

Cruising altitude of commercial jets

**1968** – the USA creates a missile that can hit multiple targets.

**1968** – the USSR creates technology to shoot down incoming missiles.

The USSR and USA followed a military strategy known as **MAD (mutual assured destruction)**. This meant they had, and were prepared to use, weapons that could wipe each other out.

# THE HUNGARIAN UPRISING, 1956

## Background of the uprising

In 1945, the Hungarian people had voted a non-communist party into power. However, a hard-line communist, Mátyás Rákosi, eventually took control by using the secret police and removing political rivals. By 1948, Rákosi was leader of Hungary, and Hungarians had little freedom. Anyone who spoke out against communism or seemed in favour of the West could be arrested.

## Khrushchev's secret speech and Imre Nagy

In February 1956, the new leader of the USSR, Nikita Khrushchev, gave a secret speech where he pledged a policy of **de-Stalinisation**, denouncing Stalin's actions and accused him of abusing human rights. He abolished the death penalty and suggested that more freedoms might be possible. Khrushchev had also talked of a '**peaceful co-existence**' with the West.

Hungarians were encouraged by Khrushchev's secret speech. They began to protest against Rákosi, who was eventually replaced by the more liberal, Imre Nagy, in October 1956. Nagy attempted to introduce some reforms, such as free elections, and demanded that Hungary leave the Warsaw Pact **(page 14)** and become neutral in the Cold War.

After Khrushchev came to power, some hoped that there might be a **thaw** in the Cold War, and relations between the superpowers might improve.

## Khrushchev's response

Khrushchev refused to allow Hungary to leave the Warsaw Pact; their withdrawal would leave a gap in the USSR's buffer zone and undermine Soviet-control. The USSR sent tanks to invade Hungary on 4th November. Many Hungarians tried to flee to Austria, but thousands were arrested, injured or killed. Nagy was arrested and executed and was replaced with the pro-Soviet János Kádár.

Soviet tanks on the streets of Budapest, Hungary in 1956.

Khrushchev's brutal treatment of Hungary sent a clear message to the other Eastern Bloc countries that disobedience to the USSR would not be tolerated.

# INTERNATIONAL REACTION TO THE SOVIET INVASION OF HUNGARY

**Many countries were critical of the Soviet invasion of Hungary, but they chose not to get involved.**

Although the West was angered by the invasion of Hungary, they weren't prepared to intervene with events in the Eastern Bloc. They didn't want to start another war, especially since it could involve nuclear weapons. The lack of involvement from the UN, NATO and the West made them look weak and ineffective.

Following Stalin's death, and the appointment of Khrushchev, some hoped that there would be an improvement in US-Soviet relations. However, the invasion of Hungary made it clear that there wouldn't be a 'thaw' in the Cold War.

> Communist supporters in the West were critical of the USSR's actions.

---

Explain **two** consequences of the Hungarian Uprising. [8]

*One consequence of the Hungarian Uprising was that other Eastern European countries realised that breaking away from the USSR would not be tolerated and any disobedience would be met with Soviet violence. Following Khrushchev's secret speech, the Hungarian people thought that they might be given more freedoms. Although Khrushchev did allow the more liberal Imre Nagy to be appointed as leader, once Nagy demanded to be released from the Warsaw Pact the USSR invaded and arrested those Hungarians who opposed communism, as well as removing Nagy and replacing him with the pro-Soviet Kádár.*

*Another consequence was that the Hungarian Uprising showed that the West was not prepared to get involved with events in the Eastern Bloc. This made the West and NATO look ineffective, especially since they had claimed they would defend countries against communism. The West avoided getting involved because they didn't want to start an outright war with the USSR since both countries possessed nuclear weapons and a nuclear war would have been devastating.*

This question should be marked in accordance with the levels-based mark scheme on page 52.

# EXAMINATION PRACTICE

**Instructions and information:**

- This page follows the format of the examination.
- The total mark for this paper is 32. The marks for each question are shown in brackets.
- You must answer Q1, Q2 and two options from Q3.
- You should allow roughly 50 minutes to answer the questions below.
- Write your answers on a separate sheet of paper using black ink.

1.  Explain **two** consequences of the formation of NATO.                                   [8]

2.  Write a narrative account analysing the key events of the Soviet invasion of Hungary in 1956.
    You may use the following in your answer:
    - Khrushchev
    - Imre Nagy
    You **must** also use information of your own.                                           [8]

3.  Explain **two** of the following:

    (i)   The importance of the Marshall Plan for the development of the Cold War.           [8]

    (ii)  The importance of the Berlin Crisis for relations between East and West.           [8]

    (iii) The importance of the arms race on superpower relations.                           [8]

# THE REFUGEE PROBLEM IN BERLIN

**Germans living in Soviet-controlled East Berlin started moving to West Berlin.**

## East v West Berlin

Although Berlin was part of East Germany and was technically communist, there were British, French and American sectors in Berlin where:

- people had more political freedom.
- capitalism was bringing greater wealth and higher standards of living.
- there was access to consumer goods which were unavailable in the Soviet-controlled part of the city.

**A sign in Berlin in English, Russian, French and German.**

## The refugee problem

The attraction of the West led to huge numbers of East Germans migrating to West Berlin through the open frontier in the city, and then on to West Germany. Between 1945 and 1961, around 3.5 million East Germans migrated from East to West Germany, out of a total population of 18 million. To make matters worse, most of the migrants were young, skilled workers whose loss had a damaging effect on the East German economy.

The East German leader, Walter Ulbricht, complained to Khrushchev that his country's economy was being destroyed. Khrushchev was also worried that the open access between West and East Berlin allowed the West to easily spy on East Germany. The mass emigration was a source of embarrassment for the Soviet Union, and also provided the West with the opportunity to claim that capitalism was more popular and successful than communism in their propaganda.

**The loss of young, skilled workers from East Germany was called the brain drain.**

## Khrushchev's Berlin Ultimatum (1958)

In 1958, Khrushchev gave a speech in Moscow where he gave the West an ultimatum. He demanded that the Western countries remove their troops from West Berlin, and that Berlin should be a "free city" controlled by the USSR.

The West refused. They believed that they needed to keep a military presence in West Berlin to protect the citizens under their control. The countries agreed to meet at a series of summits to resolve the issue.

An American cartoon showing Khrushchev as a bear. The sign reads: 'Warning! You are now leaving West Berlin!'

## Summit meetings of 1959–61

### Geneva Conference, May 1959

President Eisenhower and Khrushchev met to discuss the Berlin Ultimatum. They didn't reach an agreement, and relations remained tense.

### Camp David Summit, September 1959

The Camp David Summit was significant because it happened in the USA. The fact that Eisenhower invited Khrushchev to his country and that Khrushchev accepted, showed that the leaders were willing to co-operate. Khrushchev withdrew the Berlin Ultimatum, but he still wanted to discuss a longer-term plan for Berlin and agreed to further negotiations.

Khrushchev, Eisenhower and their wives at a state dinner, 1959.

### Paris Summit, May 1960

The summit in Paris intended to discuss:

**Nuclear weapons and a Test Ban Treaty** — both the USSR and USA knew they needed to agree to stop testing nuclear weapons to prevent radioactive damage to the Earth.

**Berlin** — the USSR wanted to stop East Germans from migrating to West Berlin.

**Cuba** — a revolution in Cuba (see **page 24**) meant that communism was dangerously close to the USA.

### The U-2 Crisis

Less than two weeks before the Paris Summit, an American U-2 spy plane was shot down over the USSR. The USA claimed that it was a weather plane, but the USSR recovered evidence from the plane that proved it was a spy plane.

When the two leaders arrived in Paris for the summit, Khrushchev demanded that the USA apologise for the spy plane. Eisenhower refused and the summit was cancelled.

A cartoon showing a Soviet fist smashing an American plane out of the sky.

This diplomatic issue meant that the two countries made no progress in discussing nuclear weapons testing, Berlin or Cuba, and tensions and suspicions escalated.

### Vienna Summit, 1961

The Vienna Summit provided another opportunity to discuss the matter of Berlin. Khrushchev decided to take a tough stance on Berlin and renewed his demand that it should become a free city and Western troops should withdraw.

Kennedy (the US President after Eisenhower) was determined not to appear weak. He called Berlin 'an island of freedom in a communist sea' and in a television broadcast said that 'We cannot, and will not, allow the Soviets to drive us out of Berlin'. To show that he meant business, he increased spending on the US military and defence spending on US troops in West Germany in case war broke out.

Kennedy and Khrushchev in 1961

---

Explain the importance of the U-2 Crisis on superpower relations.                    [8]

*Prior to the U-2 Crisis, relations between the superpowers appeared to be thawing. The Camp David Summit in 1960 was significant because Khrushchev travelled to America to meet with Eisenhower, which showed that the two were on better terms and were willing to cooperate. Khrushchev also withdrew his Berlin Ultimatum, and it seemed as though the countries could reach an amicable agreement on the matter. However, when an American spy plane was shot down over the USSR (the U-2 Crisis), relationships soured again. Eisenhower was embarrassed because he was caught in a lie (he had claimed the plane was a weather plane) and he refused to apologise, which led to Khrushchev refusing to take part in the Paris Summit. This was significant because the Paris Summit planned to address important issues such as nuclear weapons testing, migration issues in Berlin and the Cuban revolution. Following the U-2 Crisis, Khrushchev once again toughened his stance on Berlin at the Vienna Summit in 1961 and insisted that Western troops should withdraw. Kennedy refused, and months later the Berlin Wall was built.*

This question should be marked in accordance with the levels-based mark scheme on page 53.

# THE CONSTRUCTION OF THE BERLIN WALL

**In August 1961, the USSR finally acted against West Berlin.**

## The Berlin issue

The issue of Berlin remained a headache to Khrushchev:

- The migration of people from East to West Berlin causing the brain drain.
- People in East Berlin could see and access all the goods and services available to people in West Berlin which made the West, and capitalism, seem more appealing.
- Berlin was in the middle of USSR-controlled West Germany. It was an ideal place for Western spies to gather intelligence on the USSR.

## Construction, 1961

On 12th August 1961, Khrushchev began enacting his solution to the Berlin issue by building a barrier all the way around West Berlin.

Overnight, Soviet troops began constructing the barrier. At first, more than 30 miles of barbed wire was laid through the middle of Berlin, and the roads that connected East and West Berlin were torn up.

Over the next few weeks and months, the barrier was reinforced to include 15ft concrete walls and minefields, as well as hundreds of look-out towers with searchlights and machine-gun nests. The wall extended 28 miles through Berlin, and a further 75 miles around the rest of West Berlin.

The Berlin Wall around the Brandenburg Gate.

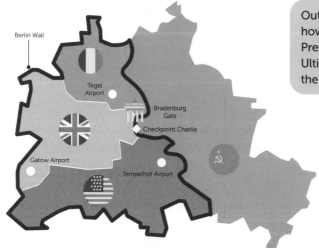

Outwardly, the West criticised the wall, however some people in the West, including President Kennedy, were relieved. The Berlin Ultimatum could have led to outright war, so the wall was seen as a more peaceful option.

# IMPACT OF THE BERLIN WALL

The wall effectively ended migration from East to West Berlin, but at a terrible cost to German citizens.

## The impact of the Berlin Wall

The wall cut off friends and families meaning for almost 30 years some parents and children never saw each other. Some East Germans were prepared to find ways to cross the border, but it was very risky. Between 1961–1989, around 5,000 East Germans escaped to West Berlin. Thousands more were arrested trying to cross and at least 130 more were shot.

The USSR viewed the Berlin Wall as a victory. They had prevented the brain drain and protected communism in East Germany.

Explain **two** consequences of the Berlin Wall.  [8]

*One consequence of the Berlin Wall was that it was no longer possible for German people to freely pass between East and West Berlin. This prevented the migration of people from Soviet-controlled East Berlin into the Western-controlled West Berlin. Although this prevented the 'brain drain' (skilled young people leaving East Berlin) it also meant that some families and loved ones were separated for 30 years.*

*Another consequence of the Berlin Wall was that it increased tensions between the superpowers. Although foreigners, such as soldiers and diplomats, were allowed to cross between East and West Berlin freely, the creation of the wall meant that security was tightened. This led to a stand-off at Checkpoint Charlie after a disagreement over travel documents and US tanks faced off against Soviet soldiers. The West also used the Wall to criticise the USSR, for example during Kennedy's visit to East Berlin, which further heightened tensions.*

This question should be marked in accordance with the levels-based mark scheme on page 52.

## Checkpoint Charlie

Foreigners, such as US troops and diplomats, were still allowed to cross, so the USSR built several checkpoints along the wall, including one called Checkpoint Charlie. In October 1961, there was a disagreement over whether Soviet troops should be permitted to check the travel documents of Americans passing through the checkpoint. On 27th October 1961, the US drove tanks up to their border at Checkpoint Charlie. The Soviets responded by sending soldiers to their side of the checkpoint. The two sides remained facing each other for 17 hours before the stand-off was ended after diplomacy talks between Kennedy and Khrushchev.

## Kennedy's visit to West Berlin

In 1963, Kennedy visited West Berlin and received a hero's welcome. Massive crowds (below) gathered to hear him give a speech where he announced his intention to protect the freedoms of West Berlin. He criticised the wall and claimed that it proved communism was so terrible that the USSR had to put up barriers to stop the citizens leaving. The USA was able to score a major propaganda victory.

# SOVIET RELATIONS WITH CUBA

Up until 1959, Cuba was on friendly terms with the USA.

## The Cuban Revolution

In 1959, the pro-American leader of Cuba, General Batista, was overthrown during a revolution. The leader of the revolution, Fidel Castro (right), travelled to the USA to meet with President Eisenhower to secure recognition for his leadership of Cuba. Eisenhower refused to meet. Instead, Castro met with representatives from the USSR who offered support to his new government. Castro had not been a communist prior to 1960, but he was attracted to communism following his involvement with the USSR. Castro's government took over all the American-owned businesses in Cuba.

Many Cubans fled to the USA during the revolution and asked the US government to overthrow Castro.

## Response from the USA and USSR

The USA felt threatened by the Cuban Revolution, Castro's ties to communism and the USSR. The USA responded by banning trade with Cuba, as America was importing Cuban sugar and tobacco. The USA hoped that this would force Castro to reconsider his actions. In January 1961, the USA broke diplomatic ties with Cuba and refused to acknowledge Castro's government.

Cuba turned to the USSR who agreed to trade with them. The USSR also sent economic aid, military equipment and technical advisors to Cuba. Khrushchev recognised the benefits of having an ally which was geographically close to the USA.

## The Bay of Pigs incident

In April 1961, newly elected President Kennedy wanted to appear tough on communism, so he decided to invade Cuba and overthrow Castro's government.

1,400 Cuban exiles who had fled to America following the revolution, were given military training and weapons, and were transported to the Bay of Pigs on the southern coast of Cuba.

Kennedy hoped that these exiles would cause an anti-communist uprising, and he promised them the support of the US Air Force. At the last minute, Kennedy withdrew his promised air support. Within two days, the exiles were easily defeated by the Cuban army. Almost 1,100 exiles were captured and ransomed to the USA in exchange for $53 million worth of food and medicine.

The USA's support for the Cuban exiles worsened superpower relations.

## Aftermath of the Bays of Pigs

The Bay of Pigs incident was a complete failure for the USA. It made Kennedy look weak and indecisive. He was determined not to repeat this failure during the Cuban Missile Crisis (**page 26**), and the incident strengthened the USA's belief in the need for containment.

Following the Bay of Pigs, the USSR and Cuba developed even closer ties, and eventually led to the USSR giving military support to Cuba which threatened the USA.

---

Write a narrative account analysing the key events leading up to the Cuban victory at the Bay of Pigs in 1961.

You **may** use the following in your answer:

- Eisenhower
- Castro

You **must** also use your own knowledge. [8]

*In 1959, Fidel Castro led a revolution in Cuba to overthrow the pro-American leader, General Batista. Castro travelled to America to try to meet with President Eisenhower to gain American recognition for his leadership of Cuba, however, Eisenhower refused to meet. Instead, Castro found an ally in the USSR who were prepared to support his new government. Although Castro had not been communist prior to the revolution, he was attracted to communism following involvement with the USSR, and he nationalised all the American-owned businesses in Cuba. America retaliated by breaking diplomatic ties with Cuba and banning trade of sugar and tobacco, but Castro just began to trade with the USSR instead. When Kennedy replaced Eisenhower as American President in 1961, he wanted to appear tough on Cuba. He decided to try to overthrow Castro with an army of 1,400 Cuban exiles who opposed Castro's leadership. These exiles were given American weapons and military training and were transported to the Bay of Pigs on the southern coast of Cuba. Kennedy hoped that these forces would generate an anti-communist uprising in Cuba, and overthrow Castro. Kennedy promised the men American air support. However, Kennedy withdrew the air support after the attack had been launched, and the exiles were easily defeated by Castro's forces in Cuba. The incident was a failure for America, and it humiliated Kennedy and made him look weak and indecisive.*

This question should be marked in accordance with the levels-based mark scheme on page 52.

---

To get top marks, you need to include information other than the bullet points in the question.

# THE CUBAN MISSILE CRISIS

The Cuban Missile Crisis was the closest the world has come to nuclear war.

## Background

The United States considered the Castro government a threat to its security. The failure of the Bay of Pigs invasion (see **page 24**) had humiliated President Kennedy and drawn Cuba closer to the Soviet Union.

Kennedy was concerned that the Soviet Union might place nuclear weapons in Cuba where they would be a direct threat to the United States. Although Khrushchev assured Kennedy that he had no intention of using Cuba to threaten the USA, this was not the case.

## Cuban missiles

Khrushchev was building a missile base in Cuba. He wanted to:
- protect Cuba (and communism) from America.
- retaliate against American missiles that were based in Turkey and pointed at the USSR.
- show his strength to the USSR and the rest of the world.

## The discovery

On 14th October 1962, a US spy plane flew over Cuba and took surveillance photographs. An analysis of the photographs showed that launch pads were being built which could be used to fire Soviet intermediate range ballistic missiles. Although the Soviet Union was already able to fire missiles into the USA from other sites, Cuba was so close the missiles could hit American cities with very little warning.

Kennedy was informed about the missile sites on 16th October but was told that, as yet, the missiles did not have nuclear warheads attached. He knew that nuclear warheads in Cuba would be a serious threat to US security and that the American public would lose faith in him if he did not act. However, if he followed the advice of some of his more aggressive advisors and bombed or invaded Cuba, this might cause a world-threatening war with the Soviet Union.

A map showing the area that nuclear missiles launched from Cuba could hit.

## The 'Thirteen Days'

The tense period between the discovery of the missile sites and the resolution of the crisis in 1962 is known as the **Thirteen Days**. During this period, there were concerns that war might break out and could lead to massive global destruction.

### 16 October

Kennedy was informed of Soviet missile sites in Cuba.

### 16–21 October

Kennedy set up **ExComm** (Executive Committee of the National Security Council) to discuss what action to take. He wanted to appear strong, but also wanted to avoid outright war. He decided to place a naval blockade around Cuba to prevent Soviet ships with nuclear warheads from docking, but he knew that the Soviet ships were already on their way.

### 22 October

Kennedy made a televised address to America to inform the public that Soviet missile sites had been discovered in Cuba, and that he was ordering a naval blockade of Cuba.

### 23 October

Khrushchev told Kennedy that his Soviet ships would break through the blockade.

### 24 October

Soviet ships approaching the blockade turned back.

### 25 October

US spy planes reported increased building work at the missile launch sites on Cuba.

### 26 October

Kennedy received a telegram from Khrushchev promising to remove the launch sites if the USA agreed not to invade Cuba.

### 27 October

Kennedy received a second telegram from Khrushchev saying that the launch sites would only be removed if the US removed its missiles in Turkey, which had been placed there to threaten the USSR. Kennedy could not openly agree to this as his NATO allies would object. So, he told Khrushchev that he would not invade Cuba and Khrushchev agreed to remove the missiles. There was no mention of the missiles in Turkey, but we now know that a secret agreement had been reached between the leaders for their removal.

### 28 October

Khrushchev agreed to remove missiles in Cuba.

Write a narrative account analysing the key events of the Cuban Missile Crisis in 1962.

You **may** use the following in your answer:

- naval blockade
- Turkey

You **must** also use your own knowledge. [8]

> On 14th October 1962, an American spy plane flying over Cuba took surveillance photographs. The photographs appeared to show that nuclear missile sites were being built on Cuba. Nuclear missiles launched from Cuba could reach a significant area of central and eastern America, so the missile sites were a real threat to the security of the USA. President Kennedy was informed on 16th October, and he created ExComm to help him decide what action to take. Although he wanted to appear strong, especially after the failure of the Bay of Pigs invasion, he also wanted to avoid war with the USSR. The photographs showed that the missiles still needed nuclear warheads, and Kennedy knew that these warheads were being shipped from the USSR to Cuba. Kennedy decided to establish a naval blockade around Cuba to prevent the missiles from reaching land. On 22nd October, Kennedy made a televised addressed to the American public informing them of the situation. There was a real danger that nuclear war could break out. Khrushchev told Kennedy that the Soviet ships would break through the American naval blockade, however once they reached the blockade, they turned back, and the threat of war was reduced. Over 26th and 27th October, Khrushchev and Kennedy corresponded to try to reach a resolution to the crisis. Khrushchev said that he would remove the launch sites in Cuba provided that America promised not to invade Cuba, and that they remove their own nuclear missiles in Turkey which were aimed at the USSR. Publicly, Kennedy agreed not to invade Cuba, and privately agreed to remove the missiles in Turkey. He knew that NATO would object to the removal of missiles in Turkey, so he had to do it secretly. After a tense thirteen days, the world was brought back from the brink of nuclear war.

*This question should be marked in accordance with the levels-based mark scheme on page 52.*

To get top marks, you need to include information other than the bullet points in the question.

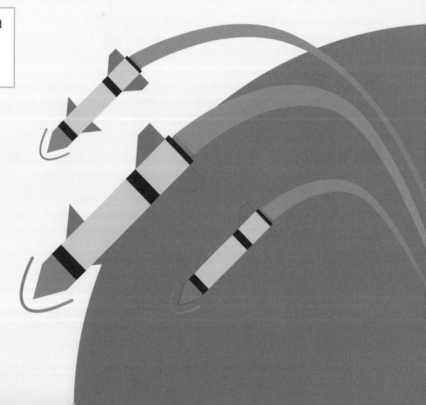

# THE CONSEQUENCES OF THE CUBAN MISSILE CRISIS

Following the Missile Crisis, relations between the superpowers improved.

## The consequences

Both Kennedy and Khrushchev claimed that they were the victor of the Cuban Missile crisis.

### Kennedy

Showed that he was a strong leader who had prevented the USSR from delivering nuclear warheads to Cuba.

### Khrushchev

Had saved Cuba from an American invasion, and protected communism. He had forced the USA to remove their missiles in Turkey.

## The 'hotline'

After the Cuban Missile Crisis, a direct line was set up between the White House (office of the American President) and the Kremlin (the office of the leader of the USSR). This **hotline** meant that the leaders could talk to each other immediately if there was an urgent matter they needed to resolve. This showed that the leaders were aware how close they had come to an outbreak of war and were prepared to co-operate to avoid it happening again.

## Attempts at arms control

### The Limited Test Ban Treaty (1963)

The failure of the Paris Summit (see **page 21**) meant that neither the USA nor the USSR had resolved the issue of nuclear weapons testing. After coming so close to nuclear war, both parties agreed to revisit the discussions, which led to the **Test Ban Treaty** in 1963, which started the process of ending nuclear weapons testing.

### The Outer Space Treaty (1967)

The Outer Space Treaty was an agreement between the USSR and the USA to only use space exploration for peaceful purposes, and that neither nation could claim territory in space. They also agreed that it should be forbidden to put nuclear weapons into space.

Soviet space exploration poster from 1964.

### The Nuclear Non-Proliferation Treaty (1968)

This treaty, signed by the USSR, the USA and 191 other countries, agreed to the peaceful use of nuclear energy and took steps towards nuclear disarmament. It agreed that only five countries could possess nuclear weapons: China, France, the USSR, the USA and the UK.

There were other reasons why the USSR and the USA wanted to de-escalate nuclear weaponry. There was some concern that nuclear weapons could be even more dangerous in the hands of other governments. Also, the more countries that possessed nuclear weapons, the less the superpowers could dominate world affairs.

---

Explain **two** consequences of the Cuban Missile Crisis. [8]

*One consequence of the Cuban Missile Crisis was that both Kennedy and Khrushchev thought they had won a victory over the other. Kennedy thought that he had successfully diffused a perilous situation and had prevented nuclear warheads from reaching Cuba. On the other hand, Khrushchev thought he had won, as he had prevented an American invasion of Cuba, and had successfully removed American nuclear weapons in Turkey. Because both leaders thought that they had won, their relationship improved, and they were more prepared to work together.*

*Another consequence of the Cuban Missile Crisis was that both the USA and the USSR realised that they had become dangerously close to nuclear war. Both the superpowers realised that they had to take action to prevent nuclear war breaking out in future. One way they did this was by establishing a direct line between the Kremlin and the White House, so that the leaders could resolve any urgent issues immediately. Another way they attempted to reduce the threat of nuclear war was by discussing the Test Ban Treaty in 1963 which began the process of ending nuclear weapons testing.*

*This question should be marked in accordance with the levels-based mark scheme on page 52.*

# OPPOSITION IN CZECHOSLOVAKIA

Czechoslovakia had been a communist satellite state since the end of World War II, but by 1968, the Czech people had had enough.

## Opposition to Soviet control in Czechoslovakia

The Czech people were unhappy with the state of their country.

Their economy was weak and was controlled by the USSR.

Czech farmers wanted to modernise their methods to improve output, but this was forbidden by the USSR.

The Czech people had few personal freedoms, and their media was censored.

The ruler of Czechoslovakia, Antonín Novotný, was a staunch supporter of the USSR and communism. He was unpopular with his people.

## The Prague Spring

The Czech people began to speak out against Soviet control.

### 1967

Czech students began protesting. Novotný asked Leonid Brezhnev (the leader of the USSR) for assistance, but he refused.

### 1968

Novotný was replaced by Alexander Dubček.

**Young Czechs celebrate during the Prague Spring, 1968.**

### April 1968

Dubček intended to introduce reforms that would give the Czech people more freedoms. Dubček wanted to:

- remove Soviet control of the economy
- lift restrictions on travel to the West
- allow freedom of speech
- allow non-communist parties to run for election.

Despite Dubček's liberal reforms, he still wanted Czechoslovakia to remain communist and he pledged to remain part of the Warsaw Pact (page 14).

Jan–Aug 1968 is known as the **Prague Spring**. It was a hopeful time for the Czech people as they thought Dubček would introduce more liberal reforms and freedoms.

# THE BREZHNEV DOCTRINE AND RE-ESTABLISHMENT OF SOVIET CONTROL

## Brezhnev's response

The USSR was concerned by Dubček's reforms, especially to allow non-communist parties to be set up. Brezhnev declared that he wouldn't allow any Eastern Bloc countries to deny communism, and he was prepared to go to war to protect communism. This became known as the **Brezhnev Doctrine** (see below). In August 1968, 200,000 troops and 2,000 tanks from the USSR, Bulgaria, Poland and Hungary invaded Czechoslovakia. The Czech people used non-violent methods to protest the invasion as they didn't want to repeat the brutality of the Hungarian Uprising (**page 16**).

Czech people protesting the USSR invasion of Czechoslovakia, August 1968. The banner reads, 'Never again with the Soviet Union!'

## The aftermath of the Prague Spring

Following the invasion, Dubček was removed from power and replaced with the pro-Soviet Gustáv Husák, who re-established Soviet control in Czechoslovakia.

A cartoon showing Dubček as a flower growing out of the dirt of Stalinism, about to be stepped on by a Soviet boot.

## The Brezhnev Doctrine

Brezhnev used his doctrine to assert control and send a clear message to other countries in the Eastern Bloc who might have been contemplating an uprising or moving away from communism.

The doctrine justified the Soviet use of military force and the removal of Dubček, which allowed the USSR to maintain control in Czechoslovakia.

The Brezhnev Doctrine ensured loyalty in the Eastern Bloc until it was abandoned during Gorbachev's leadership of the USSR (**page 44**).

# INTERNATIONAL REACTION TO SOVIET MEASURES IN CZECHOSLOVAKIA

## The consequences of the Soviet Invasion

The Soviet invasion was not popular in the communist world. It was condemned by China and by Albania and Yugoslavia, both of whom formed alliances with China. This undermined the Soviet Union's position as the leader of the communist world.

In Western Europe, communist organisations in France and Italy were so angered by the invasion that they declared themselves independent of Soviet communism.

The West condemned the use of force by the Soviet Union and accused it of acting against the wishes of the people. However, in reality, the USA considered events in Czechoslovakia a matter for the Soviet Union.

Brezhnev came to power in 1964, and the USA wanted to see what sort of leader he would be. His reaction to Czechoslovakia suggested he would be tough on the Cold War too.

Although the invasion led to President Johnson cancelling a summit meeting with Brezhnev, it had little impact on superpower relations. The USA was deeply involved in a war in Vietnam and had no intention of intervening in Czechoslovakia.

Explain **two** consequences of the invasion of Czechoslovakia. [8]

*One consequence of the invasion of Czechoslovakia was the introduction of the Brezhnev Doctrine. This doctrine stated that the USSR was willing to go to war with any country that opposed communism. Brezhnev introduced this doctrine because he was fearful that Dubček, the leader of Czechoslovakia, intended to allow free elections with non-communist parties on the ballot. The doctrine was a clear message to the other Eastern Bloc countries that opposition to communism would not be tolerated, and it probably prevented other countries from rebelling against the USSR's control.*

*Another consequence of the invasion was that it showed that America and the West were not prepared to offer military support to roll back communism in the Eastern Bloc. This lack of support probably prevented other satellite states from uprising, because they knew they couldn't count on foreign aid. This made the West, along with NATO and the UN, appear ineffective in the fight against communism although the West's unwillingness to intervene suggests that they were still fearful of an outright war with the USSR, especially since both countries possessed nuclear weapons.*

*This question should be marked in accordance with the levels-based mark scheme on page 52.*

# EXAMINATION PRACTICE

**Instructions and information:**

- This page follows the format of the examination.
- The total mark for this paper is 32. The marks for each question are shown in brackets.
- You must answer Q1, Q2 and two options from Q3.
- You should allow roughly 50 minutes to answer the questions below.
- Write your answers on a separate sheet of paper using black ink.

1. Explain **two** consequences of the Paris Summit (1960). [8]

2. Write a narrative account analysing the key events of the Prague Spring and the invasion of Czechoslovakia in 1968.

   You may use the following in your answer:
   - Dubček
   - the Brezhnev Doctrine

   You **must** also use information of your own. [8]

3. Explain **two** of the following:

   (i)   The importance of the Bay of Pigs incident on superpower relations. [8]

   (ii)  The importance of the building of the Berlin Wall on relations between East and West. [8]

   (iii) The importance of the Cuban Missile Crisis on the development of the Cold War. [8]

# DÉTENTE IN THE 1970s

During the 1970s, there was a period of **détente** (an easing of tensions).

## Reasons for détente

**To avoid nuclear war** — the Cuban Missile Crisis had brought the USA and the USSR close to nuclear war. Both countries were more prepared to cooperate to avoid this happening again.

**The arms race was expensive** — both countries wanted to use the money to improve the lives of their people instead.

**The Vietnam War** — America had been fighting communism in Vietnam since 1955. Most Americans opposed the war which had been expensive, lengthy and embarrassing. There was a feeling amongst Americans that the USA should withdraw from foreign affairs. America signed a peace treaty with Vietnam in 1973.

**Relations between China and the USSR** — China was communist, and their relationship with the USSR had panicked America. However, by the 1970s, the Sino-Soviet relationship was in decline, and relations between China and the USA had improved. Wary of being left behind, the USSR was more open to relations with the USA.

## SALT 1

Between 1972–74 Nixon and Brezhnev visited each other several times in Moscow and Washington. This showed the leaders' willingness to cooperate with each other.

In May 1972, President Nixon met with the USSR's leader, Brezhnev, in Moscow. This was significant and marked a de-escalation of tensions. While in Moscow, the two leaders took part in **Strategic Arms Limitation Talks** (**SALT**) which was a treaty to limit the numbers of ICBMs the countries possessed. SALT 1 helped to de-escalate the arms race for a period.

Nixon and Brezhnev sign the SALT 1 agreement in Moscow, 1972.

In 1975, American and Soviet astronauts shook hands in space, as a show of the increasingly friendly relations between the two countries.

## Helsinki Agreement

In 1975, 35 countries, including the USSR and the USA, signed the **Helsinki Agreement**. This treaty recognised the borders in Europe that had been established following the Second World War and meant that the West acknowledged Soviet control of territories they had gained following World War II. The treaty also laid out agreements about human rights and freedom of speech, which was a significant step towards more freedom in Soviet-controlled countries. There was also an agreement that the countries would help each other economically.

The USSR didn't uphold their agreement on improved human rights and freedom of speech. This contributed to worsening relations towards the end of the 1970s.

## SALT 2

America and the USSR entered negotiations leading towards SALT 2 between 1972–9. This aimed to limit the manufacture of nuclear weapons. An agreement was reached, and the SALT 2 treaty was signed by the new leader of the US, President Carter, and Brezhnev in 1979. However, shortly after, the USSR invaded Afghanistan (**page 37**) and the treaty was never ratified (formally approved) by the USA.

Explain **two** consequences of the Helsinki Agreement. [8]

*One consequence of the Helsinki Agreement was that it acknowledged the borders that had been established following World War II. This was significant for the Soviet Union because it gave legitimacy to their territories and meant that other countries had to recognise them. This helped to contribute to détente, because the USA signed and agreed to the borders which showed that they were willing to cooperate with the USSR.*

*Another consequence of the Helsinki Agreement was that it laid out guidelines on human rights and freedom of speech, this meant that the Soviet Union agreed to more personal freedoms in Soviet-controlled countries. This was important to the USA because it suggested that the USSR was moving away from hard-line communism and offered hope that the superpowers could reach agreements on other matters too.*

*This question should be marked in accordance with the levels-based mark scheme on page 52.*

# THE SOVIET INVASION OF AFGHANISTAN

In 1979, Soviet forces invaded Afghanistan. This invasion was a flashpoint for superpower relations and signalled the end of détente.

## Invasion

In 1978, the **PDPA** (People's Democratic Party of Afghanistan) took control of Afghanistan. The PDPA had been financed by the USSR, however there was an ideological split in the party. A pro-West faction of the PDPA overthrew the pro-Soviet faction in 1979, and Hafizullah Amin became president of Afghanistan.

Worried by the prospect of a pro-West government in Afghanistan, Brezhnev ordered an invasion and justified his actions using the Brezhnev Doctrine, President Amin was killed during a USSR attack in December. By January 1st, the USSR had established a pro-Soviet government in Afghanistan. President Carter was concerned by this invasion and considered it a threat to world peace as well as evidence that the USSR were trying to spread communism to the Middle East.

Religious groups in Afghanistan opposed communists because they suppressed the Islamic faith and tortured and executed many prominent Muslim leaders. Afghan resistance fighters created a group called the **Mujahideen**. The Mujahideen were given weapons by China and the USA and received training from American forces.

The Mujahideen rebelled against the Soviet involvement in Afghanistan, and used **guerrilla** warfare against the Red Army, such as ambushes, sabotage and hit-and-run tactics.

Mujahideen in Afghanistan, 1985 or 1986.

The Mujahideen mainly fought in the Afghan mountains which was difficult terrain for the Soviet troops. The USSR responded by using air power indiscriminately in the mountains, killing both Mujahideen fighters as well as civilians.

## The Carter Doctrine

President Carter was more hostile to the USSR than Nixon had been and was critical of the USSR's human rights abuses. In 1980, Carter announced that the USA's policy of containment (**page 9**) would include the Middle East. This is known as the **Carter Doctrine**. The USA was prepared to use force to prevent any invasions. The USA were also keen to prevent communism spreading to the Gulf states. Countries in the Gulf, such as Kuwait and Qatar, produced vast amounts of oil, and America wanted to protect its influence with these countries.

The conflict in Afghanistan lasted for 9 years, and an estimated 6-11% of the Afghan population died in the war.

## The Olympic boycotts

In 1980, the USA, along with 65 other countries, boycotted the Moscow Olympics in protest of the invasion of Afghanistan. This was embarrassing for the USSR as they had intended to use the Moscow Olympics to demonstrate the strength of communism. In 1984, the Olympics were held in Los Angeles, and the Soviet team retaliated by boycotting them.

**A cartoon protesting the Moscow 1980 Olympics, showing the Olympic rings as handcuffs.**

## The end of the war

When the new leader of the USSR, Mikhail Gorbachev (see **page 41**), was appointed in 1985, he was under significant pressure to end the war.

The war had lasted nine years. The USSR were unlikely to defeat the Mujahideen, and this was a source of embarrassment.

Soviet forces had suffered losses of 15,000 and many more had been injured.

The UN had requested that the USSR withdraw in 1980.

The war had been expensive, and the USSR couldn't afford to continue. Living standards had fallen in the USSR as a result of the war.

The USA established trade embargoes with the USSR, for example the USA had stopped sending the USSR grain.

The war made the USSR look weak, but it needed to uphold its military strength to prevent the Eastern Bloc from rebelling.

The USSR signed a peace treaty in 1988 and withdrew all remaining Soviets by 1989.

The USSR withdrawing from Afghanistan was significant. It showed that Gorbachev was willing to abandon the Brezhnev Doctrine (**page 32**).

Explain the importance of the war in Afghanistan on Cold War relations. [8]

*The Soviet invasion of Afghanistan damaged relations between the USA and the USSR. Prior to the invasion, the superpowers had been in a period of détente where relations seemed to be improving and the two countries were working together. However, President Carter saw the invasion as a threat to world peace and evidence that the USSR was trying to spread communism in the Middle East. President Carter introduced the Carter Doctrine which stated that the USA's policy of containment would now extend to the Middle East, and that the US would be prepared to use force to stop communism from spreading. The invasion effectively ended détente.*

*Prior to the invasion, the USA and USSR had signed the SALT 2 agreement, however due to the invasion in Afghanistan, the USA refused to ratify the agreement. This was a significant step back for both countries as it meant there was no limits placed on the manufacture of nuclear weapons, meaning that nuclear war was still possible.*

*The USA provided support to the Afghanistan resistance fighters, the Mujahideen, by supplying them with money, weapons and training. This led to worsening tensions, as the USA were supporting the USSR's enemy in the war.*

*The USA also placed trade embargoes on the USSR in response to the war in Afghanistan. This further damaged relations between the superpowers as this had economic repercussions on the USSR.*

*In 1980, Moscow hosted the summer Olympics. This was hoped to be a propaganda win for the USSR as they would be able to show the world the success and strength of the communist system. However, approximately 65 countries refused to participate in protest of the war in Afghanistan, which humiliated the USSR, and worsened Cold War relations, and the USSR retaliated by boycotting the 1984 Olympics.*

*This question should be marked in accordance with the levels-based mark scheme on page 53.*

# THE SIGNIFICANCE OF REAGAN AND GORBACHEV'S CHANGING ATTITUDES

The 1980s saw two new leaders, Reagan and Gorbachev. Although their relationship was strained at first, they paved the way for the end of the Cold War.

## Ronald Reagan

Reagan (below) was President of the USA between 1981–89. He was anti-communist and was initially determined to defeat the USSR in the Cold War. In a speech in 1983, Reagan described the USSR as an "evil empire" that needed "total elimination". Reagan wanted to **roll-back** communism, rather than just **contain** it.

## Second Cold War

The first few years of Reagan's presidency marked the **Second Cold War**: an increase in hostilities and military spending. In 1985, US military spending peaked at almost half a trillion dollars, £130 billion more than 1980. Reagan thought there was a 'missile gap' between the USSR and the USA and he was determined not to get left behind.

The USA developed the **neutron bomb** which could kill enemies with radiation, but the blast was minimal so there would be little damage to buildings and infrastructure. He also created new weapons such as stealth bombers (aircraft designed to avoid detection) and nuclear submarines.

## Strategic Defence Initiative (SDI)

Reagan invested in new technology. He believed that advances in technology would allow him to defeat the Soviets. In 1983, the USA began a programme called the **Strategic Defence Initiative** (**SDI**) which would allow the US to defend themselves from a ballistic missile attack. This programme was nicknamed 'Star Wars' as it planned to use satellites and lasers to destroy incoming missiles. This new technology worried the Soviets as their military weapons would become obsolete.

Some people criticised Reagan's revival of the arms race. However, it may have been a deliberate strategy to weaken the USSR. Reagan knew that the Soviet economy was on the brink of collapse, and they couldn't keep up with US military spending.

## Gorbachev

Mikhail Gorbachev (right) became leader of the USSR in 1985. Gorbachev had a very different outlook and attitude to previous leaders of the USSR. He wanted to reform the USSR and improve living standards for the Soviet people. His different attitude may have been because:

- He had attended Moscow University and was highly educated
- Gorbachev's generation were more familiar with the West.
- He was a communist, but he was more moderate and had supported Khrushchev's policy of de-Stalinisation.
- His more liberal outlook meant he had good relations with other world leaders, including Margaret Thatcher, the Prime Minister of the UK.

## Issues in the USSR

Gorbachev recognised that the USSR was struggling:

**Foreign policy —** The war in Afghanistan (see **page 37**), and the USSR's involvement with communism in Cuba meant that the USSR's military was strained.

**Economic troubles —** Living standards in the USSR were poor, and costly wars abroad plus keeping pace with American military spending, meant that Soviet money was being diverted away from the people.

**Discontentment in the Eastern Bloc —** Gorbachev realised that many countries in the Eastern Bloc wanted to break free from Soviet-control.

**Chernobyl —** In 1986, a nuclear powerplant in Chernobyl, Ukraine went into meltdown. The financial repercussions of the disaster almost bankrupted the USSR.

Despite their initial suspicions, Reagan and Gorbachev began to trust each other. Their willingness to co-operate helped to bring an end to the Cold War.

Explain the importance of the Second Cold War on superpower relations. [8]

*When Reagan became President, he wanted to be tough on communism and described the USSR as an "evil empire". Reagan also wanted to "roll back" communism, rather than just contain it. This shows that détente was over, that Reagan had little intention of cooperating with the USSR, and that he intended to be more aggressive. This initially worsened superpower relations and led to the Second Cold War.*

*One way that Reagan fuelled the Second Cold War was by increasing military spending. Reagan was concerned about a missile gap between the USSR and the USA and was worried that the USA was going to get left behind. In 1985, spending peaked at almost half a trillion dollars. He invested in new technology and weapons such as stealth bombers and nuclear submarines. This sent a strong message that the USA wanted to continue the arms race, and his intention to provoke the USSR and increase tensions.*

*Reagan also invested in new technology, such as SDI which was a defence initiative that intended to use satellites and lasers to protect the USA against ballistic missiles attacks from the Soviets. This new technology worried the Soviets as they felt that their weapons would become obsolete. Although this new technology concerned the Soviets, it also encouraged them to improve relations with the USA as they knew they couldn't keep pace with them.*

*Reagan's military spending put pressure on the USSR's economy. The USSR was already in financial difficulties following the war with Afghanistan and resolving the Chernobyl disaster. As such, Gorbachev knew that the USSR was not in a position to keep pace with US military spending, and instead tried to de-escalate tensions and look to improve relations with the USA. One way he did this was to push for nuclear arms control at the Geneva summit and sign the INF treaty. These attempts at co-operation, as well as Gorbachev's 'new thinking' helped to improve superpower relations and eventually end the Cold War.*

*This question should be marked in accordance with the levels-based mark scheme on page 53.*

# GORBACHEV'S 'NEW THINKING'

Gorbachev introduced two significant policies, **glasnost** and **perestroika**, and he also pushed for nuclear arms control.

## New thinking

### Glasnost

This policy encouraged the USSR to be more open with the West. Gorbachev also wanted to develop more freedom of speech and to eliminate corruption in the Communist Party.

In 1988, the Soviet Union allowed its citizens to access foreign radio stations, which meant they could listen to news from outside the Communist Party for the first time.

### Perestroika

This policy intended to modernise and improve the USSR by reducing military spending. Gorbachev also recognised that the USSR's economy would benefit from some small private businesses, rather than everything being state-controlled. He also permitted Soviet businesses to trade with the West.

## Summits and Treaties of the 1980s–90s

Gorbachev knew the USSR could no longer keep up with the USA in the arms race, so he took steps to reduce spending on nuclear weaponry and encouraged others to do the same.

### Geneva Summit, 1985

Reagan and Gorbachev met to discuss peace. Gorbachev was keen for the USA to stop their SDI (**page 40**).

### Intermediate-range Nuclear Force (INF) Treaty (1987)

This was a treaty signed by the USSR and the USA in 1987. Both countries agreed to reduce their medium-range missiles which could carry nuclear warheads.

Reagan and Gorbachev signing the INF treaty in 1987.

Towards the end of the 1980s, Gorbachev also withdrew Soviet troops from Afghanistan.

# GORBACHEV AND EASTERN EUROPE

Gorbachev's 'new thinking' brought about changes in the Eastern Bloc.

## The impact of Gorbachev's 'new thinking'

In 1988, Gorbachev began removing Soviet troops from Eastern Europe, partly for financial reasons. He pledged to withdraw 5,300 tanks and 50,000 Soviet troops from East Germany, Czechoslovakia and Hungary by 1990. This weakened Soviet control in the Eastern Bloc and allowed countries to speak out against communism.

Gorbachev did not intervene as Eastern Bloc countries began to loosen their ties with the USSR. This suggested that Gorbachev was abandoning the **Brezhnev Doctrine (page 32)**.

Countries were also encouraged by glasnost and more freedom of speech to democratically elect their own leaders, and break away from Soviet control.

### Poland

Free elections took place in Poland in 1989, and almost all the seats were won by the Solidarity Trade Union, a workers' rights movement.

### Hungary

The Hungarian Uprising in 1956 (**page 16**) had shown that there was anti-communist feeling in Hungary prior to Gorbachev. Once Gorbachev came to power, János Kádár was removed as leader, and free elections were held in 1989, leading to the election of a liberal president.

### Czechoslovakia

Like Hungary, Czechoslovakia had also tried to oppose communism in 1968 (**page 31**). In 1989, there were anti-communist protests, and a new president was democratically elected.

### Romania

Towards the end of 1989, a revolution led to the communist leader being overthrown. Free elections were held in 1990, which were the first in 53 years.

---

Explain **two** consequences of Gorbachev's 'new thinking' on the Eastern Bloc. [8]

*One consequence was that Gorbachev abandoned the Brezhnev Doctrine. Abandonment of the Brezhnev Doctrine meant that more Eastern Bloc countries were able to organise free elections without fear of invasion. Hungary and Poland arranged democratic elections which led to new, non-communist leaders in those countries. This weakened the control of the Soviet Union in the Eastern Bloc.*

*Another consequence of Gorbachev's 'new thinking' was that he removed Soviet forces from Eastern Bloc countries. In 1988, he pledged to remove tanks and soldiers from the satellite states. This was significant, as these countries now felt that the threat of military retaliation to protests was lessened. As a result, countries such as Romania and Czechoslovakia rebelled against communist control and overthrew communist governments.*

*This question should be marked in accordance with the levels-based mark scheme on page 52.*

# THE FALL OF THE BERLIN WALL

After almost thirty years, Berliners were finally allowed to cross the wall in 1989.

## Background

Aware of political changes in the Eastern Bloc (**page 44**), East Germans began to rebel against communism. The leader of the GDR, Erich Honecker, ordered troops to fire on protesters, but the soldiers would not. Honecker wanted Gorbachev to send Soviet reinforcements, but he refused.

Gorbachev's refusal to protect communism in East Germany was significant. It showed he had abandoned the **Brezhnev Doctrine** (**page 32**) and was no longer prepared to support communism abroad.

## The fall of the wall

In May 1989, Hungary opened its border with Austria, meaning that East Germans were able to travel to West Germany via Hungary and Austria. Thousands of Germans left the East for the West. The USSR declined to intervene in the situation.

By October, there were protests in East Germany against communism.

On November 9th 1989, gates along the Berlin Wall were opened. Although initially wary, East Berliners realised that they were being granted the freedom to cross the wall.

News spread, and delighted crowds on either side of the wall gathered to celebrate, while some tried to demolish parts of the wall. The wall was officially torn down in 1990.

Now that Berliners could pass between East and West, friends and families were reunited after 30 years.

Shortly after the fall of the wall, there were calls for East and West Germany to work together to reunify into a single country. In 1990, East and West Germany became the reunited nation of Germany.

The fall of the Berlin Wall was symbolic and encouraged other Soviet-controlled countries to rebel.

# THE COLLAPSE OF THE SOVIET UNION

Gorbachev's policies allowed Soviet-controlled countries more freedom. However, this new freedom eventually led to the collapse of the Soviet Union.

### Malta Summit

In December 1989, shortly after the fall of the Berlin Wall, US President George Bush met with Gorbachev at the Malta Summit. The superpowers discussed the changes happening in Europe and the lifting of the Iron Curtain (**page 8**). The two leaders announced an end to the Cold War.

### Collapse

Between 1990–1992, 14 former Soviet Republics, including Lithuania, Latvia, Estonia and Georgia, declared themselves independent, and left the USSR. The USA recognised their independence.

In 1990, Gorbachev faced criticism from both his supporters and his opponents. Supporters thought his reforms hadn't gone far enough and his opponents were angry at the collapse of Soviet control.

Hard-line communists plotted a coup to overthrow Gorbachev in August 1991. However, the coup failed, and there were protests against communism.

The USSR was dissolved in December 1991, and the Soviet Union became the Russian Federation led by Boris Yeltsin. Yeltsin transformed Russia into a capitalist country.

Following political changes in the Eastern Bloc (**page 44**), the Warsaw Pact officially ended in 1991. This ended the military alliance between the members of the Pact.

Explain **two** consequences of the collapse of the Soviet Union. [8]

*One consequence of the collapse of the Soviet Union was that countries from the USSR began to declare independence. For example, between 1990–91, 14 republics left the USSR and their independence was recognised internationally. This meant that the size of the USSR's territories decreased, and its sphere of influence was reduced.*

*A second consequence was that the Warsaw Pact was officially ended in February 1991. The end of this pact meant that there was no longer a military alliance between the USSR and the Eastern Bloc countries. This meant that previous members of the Warsaw Pact felt more confident in gaining independence from the USSR as there would no longer be the threat of military action.*

This question should be marked in accordance with the levels-based mark scheme on page 52.

# EXAMINATION PRACTICE

---

**Instructions and information:**

- This page follows the format of the examination.
- The total mark for this paper is 32. The marks for each question are shown in brackets.
- You must answer Q1, Q2 and two options from Q3.
- You should allow roughly 50 minutes to answer the questions below.
- Write your answers on a separate sheet of paper using black ink.

---

1.  Explain **two** consequences of the fall of the Berlin Wall.                     [8]

2.  Write a narrative account analysing the events following the Soviet invasion of Afghanistan between 1979–84.

    You may use the following in your answer:
    - the Mujahideen
    - the Olympic boycotts

    You **must** also use your own information.                     [8]

3.  Explain **two** of the following:

    (i)   The importance of Gorbachev's 'new thinking' on the Cold War.                     [8]

    (ii)  The importance of Ronald Reagan on superpower relations.                     [8]

    (iii) The importance of détente on superpower relations.                     [8]

# EXAMINATION PRACTICE ANSWERS

Key Topic 1

1.  One consequence of the formation of NATO was that it strengthened the alliances in the West. NATO was a military agreement between the USA, Britain, Canada and several western European countries that agreed that if one of the member states came under attack, the other member states would intervene to protect it. This created a powerful group of capitalist countries willing to defend each other.

    A second consequence of the formation of NATO was that it threatened the USSR. The USSR responded to this threat by creating an equivalent agreement amongst communist countries, called the Warsaw Pact. This Pact agreed that if any members of the Warsaw Pact were invaded, the other members would help protect it. This meant that countries were encouraged to pick a side, which resulted in two opposing organisations willing to go to war with each other if their members came under attack.

2.  After World War II, Hungary had a non-communist leader, however within a few years, he was overthrown by the hard-line communist, Rákosi. The Hungarian people were unhappy with life under Rákosi, as they had few personal freedoms, and could be persecuted for speaking out against communism. In February 1956, the leader of the USSR, Khrushchev gave a secret speech which proposed a policy of de-Stalinisation allowing more personal freedoms. The Hungarian people were encouraged by this, and protested Rákosi. Initially, the USSR seemed willing to listen to the Hungarian people, and the more moderate Imre Nagy became the leader of Hungary. Nagy proposed some liberal reforms such as free elections and leaving the Warsaw Pact, so that Hungary would be a neutral country in the Cold War. However, Khrushchev was not willing to allow free elections, as this undermined Soviet control. He was also unprepared to allow Hungary to leave the Warsaw Pact as this would leave a gap in the USSR's buffer zone – a bloc of countries on its western border used to protect the USSR from the West. Khrushchev did not want other countries in the USSR or Eastern Bloc to follow Hungary's example, so in November 1956, Khrushchev ordered Soviet tanks and soldiers to invade Hungary. Hungarians tried to flee to Austria, but many were arrested or killed. Nagy was captured and executed and was replaced by the pro-Soviet Kádár. The Hungarian invasion sent a strong message to other Eastern Bloc countries who were contemplating loosening ties with the Soviet Union which demonstrated that disobedience would be punished.

3.  (i)  Many European countries had been devastated by World War II, and their economies had suffered. The USA were concerned that these economic hardships would cause an increase in communist support in Europe as people looked for solutions to their economic problems. The USA were following a policy of containment, where they were desperate to stop communism from spreading. In order to do this, General Marshall suggested that the USA promise $12 billion of aid to European countries to help them rebuild and recover after the war. This was known as the Marshall Plan. The Marshall Plan caused tensions to increase between the superpowers as the USSR saw it as the USA trying to buy Europe's loyalty and they also viewed the USA's policy of containment as an attack on communism. The USSR forbade its satellite states from accepting aid, as the USSR didn't want the Eastern Bloc to benefit from capitalism. Instead, the USSR introduced the Molotov Plan to provide aid to the Eastern Bloc countries that had been forbidden from receiving Marshall Plan aid. Overall, the Marshall Plan caused an escalation in Cold War tensions as each of the superpowers tried to prove that their ideology would help European countries recover after World War II. The Marshall Plan created allies for the USA in Europe, and the Molotov Plan kept Eastern Bloc countries loyal. This helped to reinforce the two opposing sides of the Cold War, which eventually led to the formation of NATO and the Warsaw Pact.

3.  (ii)  The Berlin Crisis was an important event for relations between East and West because it marked the first outward show of hostilities between the superpowers and proved that the USSR was prepared to go to extreme lengths to try to assert control in Berlin. The USSR restricted land access to West Berlin in the hope that the West would withdraw from their zones in the capital. The Berlin Blockade meant that people living in the Western-controlled part of Berlin faced a shortage of food and medicine, which showed that the USSR was prepared to starve Berliners in order to gain control of Berlin. The western powers decided to fly supplies into Berlin, and they continued to do this for 11 months at a cost of $224 million. This showed that the West weren't prepared to give in to the USSR's demands at any cost. This retaliation and stubbornness was characteristic of the Cold War. Eventually, the USSR lifted the Berlin Blockade which was seen as a source of humiliation for Stalin and a victory for the West, which increased tensions further. The USSR's actions also demonstrated to the German people what the USSR was prepared to do in order to maintain control. As a result, many Germans in Soviet-controlled areas began migrating to Western areas. This migration was a source of frustration to the USSR, as it suggested that Germans preferred capitalism to communism. This eventually led to tensions over Berlin worsening and the building of the Berlin Wall.

3.    (iii)   The arms race began when the USA developed the atomic bomb in the 1940s. Truman was keen to tell Stalin about the USA's nuclear weapons at the Potsdam Conference, as he thought that it would frighten the USSR and give him a military advantage. Stalin viewed Truman's actions as the USA trying to intimidate the USSR, and as a result, Stalin was even more determined to create a pro-Soviet buffer zone in Eastern Europe, which contributed to worsening tensions between the two superpowers. The USSR also responded by developing their own atomic weapons a few years later in 1949. This retaliation was characteristic of the arms race and led to each country developing more sophisticated weaponry to out-do each other such as Hydrogen bombs and ICBMs. This competition meant that the superpowers were extremely distrustful of each other, and led to worsening relations. The arms race ensured that the USA and the USSR were both following a military strategy known as mutual assured destruction, which meant that each country was prepared to not only wipe their rival out, but also themselves. While the development of the arms race showed the increasing hostilities between the superpowers, it also meant that the superpowers were reluctant to declare war on each other, as they knew it could lead to a devastating nuclear war. For example, when the USSR invaded Hungary in 1956, the West and NATO declined to get involved. They feared that any involvement could cause nuclear war.

## Key Topic 2

1.    One consequence of the Paris Summit was, that after a brief improvement in superpower relations, the USSR and the USA once again became more hostile towards each other. These hostilities began following the U-2 Crisis when a US spy plane was shot down by the USSR. At the summit, Eisenhower refused to apologise to Khrushchev for spying on the USSR, and Khrushchev refused to take part in the summit. This souring of relations contributed to increasing tensions and suspicions between the two nations.

      A second consequence of the Paris Summit was that because the summit was cancelled, important issues that were due to be discussed were not resolved. For example, the leaders intended to discuss migration issues in Berlin, and prior to the U-2 Crisis it seemed as though a satisfactory resolution could be reached. However, because these matters weren't discussed, Khrushchev hardened his stance on the Berlin Ultimatum at the Vienna Summit in 1961, and his reluctance to negotiate eventually led to the building of the Berlin Wall.

2.    The Czech people were very unhappy with how their country was being run. Their leader, Novotny, was a hard-line communist supporter and his leadership was very unpopular. For example, the Czech economy was weak, the Czech people had few personal freedoms and their media was censored. In 1967, Czech students began a protest against Novotny. Novotny asked for help from the USSR in dealing with the protesters, but Brezhnev refused. In 1968, Novotny was replaced by the more liberal Alexander Dubček. This marked the start of the Prague Spring, a hopeful time for the Czech people, as they believed that Dubček would introduce more moderate policies. Dubček planned to lessen USSR control of the Czech economy and allow non-communist parties to run in elections. The USSR were resistant to Dubček's reforms – especially allowing non-communists to run for election. If non-communist parties won in an election, this would undermine Soviet-control, and Brezhnev was determined not to let this happen in Czechoslovakia or any other satellite states. As a result, he introduced the Brezhnev Doctrine, which stipulated that the USSR was prepared to go to war to protect communism. Consequently, 200,000 troops and 2,000 tanks from Bulgaria, Poland and Hungary invaded Czechoslovakia. The Czech people wanted to avoid the violence of the Hungarian Uprising, so their resistance to the invasion was largely peaceful and non-violent. This meant that the USSR easily regained control. Dubček was removed, and the pro-Soviet Husák was installed as the leader of Czechoslovakia to ensure loyalty to the USSR. The Soviet invasion of Czechoslovakia served as a warning to any other Eastern Bloc countries who were thinking of loosening ties with the USSR, as the Brezhnev Doctrine ensured that defiance would be met with military intervention.

3.    (i)   The Bay of Pigs incident led to worsening relations between the superpowers. President Kennedy had just been elected, so he was keen to appear tough on the revolution in Cuba and their relationship with the USSR. Kennedy believed that the USA could overthrow the Cuban government using 1,400 Cuban exiles, who had fled to the USA once Castro had come to power. Kennedy gave these exiles American weapons and military training and intended to transport them to the Bay of Pigs where he hoped they would start an uprising against Castro. This uprising would be bolstered by US air support. This worsened relations between the USSR and the USA, as it showed that the USA were prepared to use force against communism in Cuba. However, the invasion was a disaster. Kennedy removed the air support he had promised the exiles, and they were easily captured by Castro's revolutionary forces. The incident was a source of humiliation for Kennedy and his failure to commit to the uprising made him look indecisive. This had the effect of toughening Kennedy's attitude towards the USSR and Cuba and meant that he was determined not to appear weak during the Cuban Missile Crisis. It also strengthened Kennedy's belief in the need for a containment policy. The Bay of Pigs incident strengthened the ties between Cuba and the USSR, which made the USA feel threatened and worsened relations between the superpowers.

3. (ii) The building of the Berlin Wall led to worsening relations between East and West. Prior to the building of the Wall, the superpowers had been attempting to discuss Khrushchev's Berlin Ultimatum and to work towards a resolution that would satisfy everyone. However, following the breakdown of the Paris Summit in 1960, Khrushchev toughened his stance on Berlin. Khrushchev took matters into his own hands and began building the Berlin Wall overnight on 12th August 1961. The Berlin Wall was a reaction to East Berliners migrating into West Berlin, as well as East Berliners having access to the goods and services in capitalist West Berlin. The construction of the wall showed that Khrushchev wanted to maintain control of the people of East Berlin, and that he felt threatened by the West and the appeal of capitalism. The Berlin Wall also led to stand-offs between Soviet troops and Western troops, which further showed the heightened tensions between the two superpowers. For example, the stand-off at Checkpoint Charlie in October 1961 lasted 17 hours and was only called off following talks between Kennedy and Khrushchev. This shows that there were hostilities between Soviet and American troops in Berlin, as well as between the leaders of the superpowers. Kennedy used the Berlin Wall as a source of pro-capitalist propaganda during his trip to Berlin in 1963. He claimed that the wall had been built because communism was so terrible Khrushchev needed to prevent East Berliners from leaving. This public denouncement of the Berlin Wall angered Khrushchev and worsened relations.

3. (iii) The Cuban Missile Crisis was significant for the development of the Cold War because it was the closest the world had come to nuclear war. Kennedy was concerned that the USSR was using Cuba as a base to launch nuclear weapons at America. Although Khrushchev assured Kennedy this wasn't the case, he was lying. In October 1962, an American spy plane identified that the USSR were in fact building missile bases in Cuba. This proved that Khrushchev had been lying and increased the mistrust between the two superpowers. The missiles did not yet have nuclear warheads, but Kennedy knew that Soviet ships were on their way to Cuba. This showed the threat that the USSR posed to the USA, as nuclear missiles launched from Cuba could reach most of central and eastern America. Kennedy knew that he needed to take action in order to prevent the warheads from reaching Cuba, so he proposed a naval blockade around Cuba. He announced his plans for the naval blockade in a television broadcast to the public. This was significant because the American public were aware of just how far tensions had escalated and how close the country was to the outbreak of war. Khrushchev initially refused to tell his ships carrying the warheads to turn around, which suggested that he was determined for the warheads to reach Cuba at any cost, however, on the 24th October, the Soviet ships retreated. Following this, Kennedy and Khrushchev corresponded and reached an agreement. Kennedy promised not to invade Cuba, and secretly agreed to remove US missiles in Turkey that were a direct threat to the USSR. In return the USSR agreed to remove missiles in Cuba. Following the Cuban Missile Crisis, relations between the superpowers improved. Both realised how close they had come to nuclear war and took steps to prevent it from happening again. They set up a direct line between the Kremlin and the White House so that both leaders could talk directly to each other if anything urgent happened, and they both took steps towards limiting nuclear weapons testing with the Limited Test Ban Treaty of 1963.

## Key Topic 3

1. One consequence of the fall of the Berlin Wall was that it encouraged other Soviet-controlled countries to call for their independence. Prior to the fall of the Berlin Wall, Gorbachev had refused to support the leader of the GDR with Soviet reinforcements against rebellions in Eastern Berlin. This suggested that Gorbachev had abandoned the Brezhnev Doctrine and wasn't prepared to intervene in uprisings. As such, during 1989–91, the majority of Soviet-controlled republics and satellite states rebelled against Soviet control and gained their independence.

   Another consequence of the fall of the Berlin Wall was the reunification of Berlin, which allowed separated families and friends to see each other for the first time in almost 30 years. Following the freedom of movement in Berlin, there were further calls to reunify the whole of Germany, which had been split into East and West Germany following Germany's defeat in the Second World War. The country was unified into the nation of Germany in 1990.

2. In 1978, the Soviet-financed PDPA took control of Afghanistan. However, there was an ideological split in the group with a pro-Soviet faction and a pro-West faction. Eventually the pro-West faction overthrew the pro-Soviet group. This concerned Brezhnev, as he didn't want Afghanistan to fall to the West. As a result, he called for a Soviet invasion of Afghanistan, where the pro-Western leader of the PDPA was killed and replaced with a pro-Soviet government. These actions concerned the USA, who were committed to a policy of containment, and they were worried that communism could spread through the Middle East. This led to President Carter introducing the Carter Doctrine, which stated that America would get involved in the Middle East in order to prevent communism from spreading there. Within Afghanistan, a resistance group called the Mujahideen formed. This group opposed the persecution of Muslims by communists and began guerrilla warfare against the Soviet and pro-Soviet forces in Afghanistan. The USA, along with China, provided funds, weapons and training to the Mujahideen, to help their fight against the Soviets. The war in Afghanistan was very controversial globally, and more than 60 countries objected to the war by boycotting the Moscow Olympics in 1980. This was embarrassing for the USSR, as they had hoped to use the Olympics as a way to promote the strength of communism to people abroad, but this was overshadowed by the boycotts. Angered by this, the USSR, along with other Soviet-controlled countries, boycotted the Olympics hosted in the USA in 1984.

3    (i)    Gorbachev's 'new thinking' was an instrumental part in the collapse of the Soviet Union and the end of the Cold War. When Gorbachev came to power, he realised that the USSR was facing serious problems. The USSR's economy was suffering. Expensive wars abroad plus keeping up with the arms race meant that living standards in the USSR were poor. He also recognised that there was discontent in the Eastern Bloc and many countries were keen to break free from Soviet control. As a result, he introduced 'new thinking' to try to fix these problems. His policy of glasnost encouraged the USSR to be more open with the West and for more freedom of speech. This resulted in more Soviet-controlled countries speaking out against the USSR and began a chain reaction of uprisings which led to Soviet republics and satellite states loosening ties with the USSR and gaining their independence. These countries felt more confident in attempting these uprisings because Gorbachev seemed to have abandoned the Brezhnev Doctrine, which had called for invasions of any Soviet-controlled countries which had tried to renounce the USSR. Another element of Gorbachev's new thinking was to stop participating in the arms race, as he realised that it was expensive and damaging the USSR's economy. As well as this, Gorbachev also encouraged the USA to limit its own nuclear weapons at the Geneva Summit and negotiations over the INF treaty which limited the medium-range missiles each country owned. This willingness to de-escalate nuclear weaponry helped to contribute to improved relations between the superpowers. By 1989, Gorbachev and Bush's relationship had improved to the point where they were prepared to declare the end of the Cold War.

3.   (ii)   Ronald Reagan was very influential on superpower relations. Initially, Reagan worsened superpower relations. When he was first elected, he was very outspoken against the Soviet Union calling them "an evil empire". This would have increased tensions between the superpowers. Tensions were further increased when Reagan increased military spending and reignited the arms race by funding research into new weapons, such as stealth bombers and nuclear submarines. This threatened the USSR. This period of Reagan's presidency was marked by the Second Cold War, which saw an escalation of tensions. However, once Gorbachev came to power, relations between the superpowers began to improve. Reagan was more willing to work with Gorbachev because he had more liberal ideas, and other world leaders, such as Margaret Thatcher, were prepared to work with him. Reagan also recognised that Gorbachev was willing to make changes to the USSR with his policies of glasnost (openness with the West) and perestroika (economic reforms). Consequently, when Gorbachev wanted to negotiate a reduction in nuclear arms spending, Reagan was more prepared to cooperate, and the two leaders met and signed the INF Treaty which agreed that the countries would reduce their number of medium-range missiles. This willingness to co-operate was inherited by President Bush, who along with Gorbachev, announced the end of the Cold War in 1989.

3.   (iii)  The period of détente marked an improvement in the relationship between the USSR and the USA during the Cold War. Détente had been brought about because both superpowers recognised that the Cold War was a drain on money and resources, so both superpowers were more willing to cooperate. Both countries were prepared to de-escalate the arms race, as the money could be better spent improving the lives of their citizens, and Nixon and Brezhnev met in Moscow to take part in SALT I which was a negotiation to limit the number of ICBMs the two countries had. This was important, as both the USSR and USA were prepared to reduce military spending which suggested that they wanted to improve relations. Furthermore, Nixon and Brezhnev made efforts to work on their relationship, and both leaders went to each other's country which was a massive step forward in terms of showing a willingness to cooperate. The Helsinki Agreement was also an important part of détente which helped to improve relations. For the Soviet Union, countries recognised the USSR's borders which had changed following World War II. This pleased the USSR at it gave their territories and sphere of influence more recognition. For the USA, the Helsinki Agreement was significant because Brezhnev agreed to better human rights and freedom of speech in Soviet-controlled countries. This was important for America as it showed a willingness for the USSR to move away from some of its more hard-line communist policies. Both countries were willing to take part in propaganda to demonstrate their improving relations. For example in 1975, American and Soviet astronauts shook hands in space which was a symbolic show of friendship between the two countries. The countries also agreed to SALT 2, a treaty which aimed to limit the manufacture of nuclear weapons. While this was another example of détente improving relations, it was short lived, as the treaty was never ratified by the USA following the Soviet invasion of Afghanistan. This invasion marked the end of détente and the beginning of increasing tensions between the superpowers.

# LEVELS-BASED MARK SCHEMES FOR EXTENDED RESPONSE QUESTIONS

Questions 1, 2 and 3 require extended writing and use mark bands. Each answer will be assessed against the mark bands, and a mark is awarded based on the mark band it fits into.

The descriptors have been written in simple language to give an indication of the expectations of each mark band. See the Edexcel website for the official mark schemes used.

## Question 1

This question is worth 8 marks. You are asked to give two consequences and each will be marked out of 4 using the following table.

| Level 2 (3–4 marks) | • The answer analyses a feature and gives a consequence. <br> • The answer gives specific information about the topic to support the explanation which shows good knowledge of the period. |
|---|---|
| Level 1 (1–2 marks) | • The answer gives a simple comment about a consequence. <br> • The answer gives generalised information about the topic, which shows limited knowledge of the period. |
| 0 marks | • No answer has been given or the answer given makes no relevant points. |

## Question 2

| Level 3 (6–8 marks) | • The answer gives a clear narrative which is well organised and sequential and leads to an outcome. The answer demonstrates and analyses clear links between the events. <br> • The answer includes accurate and relevant information, which shows good knowledge and understanding. <br> • The answer includes information which goes beyond the stimulus points given in the question. |
|---|---|
| Level 2 (3–5 marks) | • The answer gives a narrative which shows some organisation and leads to an outcome. The answer demonstrates and analyses some links between the events but may lack coherence. <br> • The answer includes accurate and relevant information, which shows some knowledge and understanding. |
| Level 1 (1–2 marks) | • The answer gives a simple narrative, with limited analysis and organisation. <br> • The answer includes limited knowledge and understanding. |
| 0 marks | • No answer has been given or the answer given makes no relevant points. |

## Question 3

This question is worth 16 marks. You will be asked to explain the importance of two events and each will be marked out of 8.

| Level 3<br>(6–8 marks) | • The answer gives an explanation which shows analysis of importance. It demonstrates reasoning that is clear and well structured.<br>• The answer includes accurate and relevant information, which shows good knowledge and understanding. |
|---|---|
| Level 2<br>(3–5 marks) | • The answer gives an explanation which shows an attempt to analyse the importance. It demonstrates some reasoning, but some passages may lack clarity and organisation.<br>• The answer includes accurate and relevant information, which shows some knowledge and understanding. |
| Level 1<br>(1–2 marks) | • The answer gives a simple explanation, with limited development and organisation.<br>• The answer includes limited knowledge and understanding. |
| 0 marks | • No answer has been given or the answer given makes no relevant points. |

# INDEX

## N

Nagy, Imre  16
NATO  10, 14, 17, 27
Nixon  35, 37
neutron bomb  40
Novikov telegram  7
Novotny, Antonin  31
Nuclear Non-Proliferation
    Treaty  30
nuclear powerplant  41

## O

Olympic boycotts  38
Outer Space Treaty  30

## P

Paris Summit  20, 21, 30
PDPA  37
peaceful co-existence  16
perestroika  43
Potsdam Conference  3, 7
Prague Spring  31, 32
President Carter  36, 37
President Johnson  33
President Kennedy  21, 22, 23,
    24, 25, 26, 27, 29, 30
President Nixon  35, 37

## R

Rákosi, Mátyás  16
Reagan, Ronald  40, 43
Red Army  2, 37
refugee problem  13, 19
reparations  2, 3
Ronald Reagan  40, 43

## S

SALT 1  35
SALT 2  36
satellite states  8, 9
Second Cold War  40
Soviet invasion
    of Afghanistan  37
    of Czechoslovakia  32
    of Hungary  17
Soviet satellite states  8
Soviet Union collapse  46
sphere of influence  8, 10
Stalin, Joseph  2, 3, 5, 7, 8, 10, 12
Strategic Defence Initiative
    (SDI)  40, 43
summit meetings of 1959-61
    20, 21
superpowers  5

## T

Tehran Conference  2
Test Ban Treaty  20, 30
Thirteen Days  27
Truman Doctrine  9, 10
Truman, Harry S  5, 7, 9
Turkey  14, 26, 27, 28, 29

## U

U-2 Crisis  21
United Nations  2

## V

Vienna Summit  21

## W

Warsaw Pact  14, 16, 31
    end of  46
West Berlin  13, 19, 20, 22, 23
West Germany  12, 13, 19, 22, 45
Winston Churchill  5, 8

## Y

Yalta Conference  2
Yeltsin, Boris  46

# ACKNOWLEDGEMENTS

**The questions in the ClearRevise textbook are the sole responsibility of the authors and have neither been provided nor approved by the examination board.**

Every effort has been made to trace and acknowledge ownership of copyright. The publishers will be happy to make any future amendments with copyright owners that it has not been possible to contact. The publisher would like to thank the following companies and individuals who granted permission for the use of their images and extracts in this textbook.

All graphics and images not mentioned below © Shutterstock

Images on page 4 — (Is this tomorrow) — Creative Commons Attribution-ShareAlike 4.0 International License (CC BY-SA 4.0)
— Russian communist Anti-capitalist propaganda poster 'Capital' by Victor Deni © Alamy Stock Photo / World History Archive

Images on page 5 — (Truman) — Truman © Arkady Mazor / Shutterstock
— (Churchill) — Churchill © Olga Popova / Shutterstock

Image on page 8 — public domain, Polona

Image on page 9 — German metal plaque Post War propaganda European Cooperation for the MARSHALL PLAN © Alamy Stock Photo / ARCHIVIO GBB

Image on page 10 — 'The New Imperialism.' American cartoon, 1951, by D. R. Fitzpatrick © Alamy Stock Photo / GRANGER - Historical Picture Archive

Image on page 13 — public domain, United States Air Force Historical Research Agency

Image on page 14 — Banner of the Non-Soviet Union: American cartoon by D. R. Fitzpatrick, 1949 © Alamy Stock Photo / GRANGER - Historical Picture Archvie

Images on page 15 — (Hydrogen bomb) — public domain, U.S. Department of Energy, 1952
— (missile) — public domain, US Navy

Image on page 16 — public domain, FORTEPAN / Nagy Gyula

Image on page 20 — Again Berlin - again the bear © Alamy Stock Photo / Album
— (Khrushchev and Eisenhower) — public domain, Dwight D. Eisenhower Presidential Library

Image on page 21 — (cartoon) — U-2 Image © Art Villone / Shutterstock
— (Kennedy and Khrushchev) — public domain, The John F. Kennedy Presidential Library and Museum

Image on page 23 — public domain, The John F. Kennedy Presidential Library and Museum

Image on page 24 — Castro © emkaplin / Shutterstock

Image on page 30 — Vintage Soviet Space Race Propaganda Poster © Alamy Stock Photo / JJs

Image on page 31 — The Prague Spring, Czechoslovakia, 1968 © Alamy Stock Photo / The Print Collector

Image on page 32 — Czech protest, 1968 © Alamy Stock Photo / GRANGER - Historical Picture Archive

Image on page 32 — A blow to imperialism by Fritz Behrendt © Alamy Stock Photo / Album

Image on page 35 — public domain, The Richard Nixon Presidential Library and Museum

Image on page 37 — Afganistan 1985-1986 © Alamy Stock Photo / Russian Look Ltd.

Image on page 38 — Moscow Olympics 1980 © Alamy Stock Photo / Album

Image on page 40 — Reagan © mark reinstein / Shutterstock

Image on page 41 — Gorbachev after headliners coup attempt August 1991 © Alamy Stock Photo / Nikolai Ignatiev

Image on page 43 — public domain, The Ronald Reagan Library

Image on page 45 — Fall of the Berlin Wall © Alamy Stock Photo / Agencja Fotograficzna Caro

# EXAMINATION TIPS

With your examination practice, use a boundary approximation using the following table. These boundaries have been calculated as an average across past History papers rather than an average of this paper. Be aware that the grade boundaries can vary quite a lot from year to year, so they should be used as a guide only.

| Grade | 9 | 8 | 7 | 6 | 5 | 4 | 3 | 2 | 1 |
|---|---|---|---|---|---|---|---|---|---|
| Boundary | 83% | 75% | 67% | 58% | 51% | 42% | 30% | 19% | 8% |

1. Read the questions carefully. Don't give an answer to a question that you *think* is appearing (or wish was appearing!) rather than the actual question.

2. Make sure your handwriting is legible. The examiner can't award you marks if they can't read what you've written.

3. Each question in this paper is worth 8 marks, so use your time evenly.

4. Make sure you know the dates each superpower leader was in charge in the period 1941–91, and which of the key events they were responsible for.

5. When answering Q1, your explanation should show the link between the event and the consequence, don't just describe something that happened after the event.

6. For Q2, only write about events during the date range given in the question. You won't get marks for describing something that happened before or after.

7. When writing your answers to Q2, make sure your narrative response has a beginning, a middle and an end, but don't write your response in the first person or as a story. A historical narrative needs to be factual, rather than emotional.

8. Read the options for Q3 carefully to ensure you are selecting the correct content for your answer.

9. Use linking words and phrases to show you are developing your points or comparing information, for example, "as a consequence", "this shows that" and "on the other hand". This helps to give your answer structure, and makes it easier for the examiner to award you marks.

10. If you need extra paper, make sure you clearly signal that your answer is continued elsewhere. Remember that longer answers don't necessarily score more highly than shorter, more concise answers.

11. Try to save five minutes at the end of the exam to check over your answers and spot any obvious mistakes.

**Good luck!**

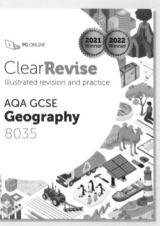
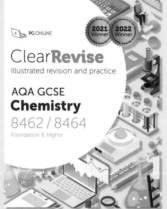
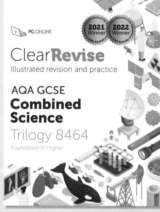

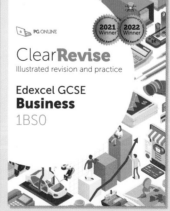
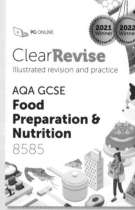